The Best from New Mexico Kitchens

New Mexico Magazine's

The Best
from
New Mexico Kitchens

by
Sheila MacNiven Cameron

Drawings by Larry King,
Richard Sandoval, Jim Wood.

New Mexico Magazine, Santa Fe, NM
USA

Also by Sheila MacNiven Cameron
The Highlander's Cookbook
Homemade Ice Creams and Sherbets

First paperback edition 1978
by *New Mexico Magazine*

Copyright © 1978 by *New Mexico Magazine*

Published by *New Mexico Magazine*

ISBN 0-937206-35-0

New Mexico Magazine
495 Old Santa Fe Trail
Santa Fe, New Mexico 87501

Library of Congress Catalog Card Number
78-73806

17th Printing, February 2000

Designed by Richard C. Sandoval

cover photo by Steve Larese
cover design Bette Brodsky

Food, courtesy of Florence Jaramillo and Rancho de Chimayó, includes (clockwise from top): sopaipillas; guacamole dip; combo plate with green-chile chicken enchilada, taco, tamale, beans and Spanish rice; carne adovada with posole and beans; stuffed sopaipilla with guacamole; Chimayó cocktail.

CONTENTS

INTRODUCTION

There are those who call it Mexican cooking. But it's not the same as the cooking south of the border. Or east or west of the border, either.

New Mexican cooking is unique to New Mexico. The stacked enchiladas topped with an egg and smothered in thick red sauce, the tender sopaipillas, the posole stew, rich and meaty, the green chile and blue corn tortillas — these are typically New Mexican dishes.

Most "Mexican" cooking is essentially Indian, as adapted by the Spanish. In New Mexico, the cooking therefore was originally based on Pueblo Indian dishes and on the foods grown by these people — and not on the foods prepared by the Indians of Mexico.

But it was more than that, of course. As time went on, there were influences from Mexico, from France, from Britain, from the Eastern Seaboard colonies. The cowboy and the trader contributed to the cuisine as did the railroader, the artist and the scientist. And today, New Mexico kitchens, in typical Southwestern fashion, turn out a rich variety of dishes — from chuckwagon specialties to haute cuisine.

But always there is that special dash, that New Mexican fillip that turns a commonplace dish into the sensational. Green chile in green pea soup. Fresh corn in a quiche. Red chile powder in a Yorkshire pudding. Cheese in a bread pudding.

A number of the recipes in this book have appeared in past issues of **New Mexico Magazine,** but many others have never before been in print. Some come from the kitchens of New Mexico restaurants. Most, however, come from home kitchens, where good cooks daily turn out those tasty, economical and healthful dishes that make the taste buds tingle and leave the appetite unsatisfied with lesser offerings.

CHILE —
NEW MEXICO'S
FIERY SOUL

by John Crenshaw

To my knowledge, no one has ever died from an overdose of 8-Methyl-N-vanillyl-6-nonenamide, although countless thousands have known the symptoms of gastronomic flashbacks.

The substance may be addictive; although there are no severe withdrawal symptoms, its prolonged absence leaves regular users with a vague, empty feeling located nearer the soul than other, more definable areas of the physical body. The substance, become more symbolic than curative, stirs memories and longing: old friends and red wine, close families at dinner, fields of deep green wetted by the Rio Grande's muddy waters.

Simply put, it's homesickness, a yearning focused on a particular chemical that for many is a way of life. The sufferer is likely a displaced New Mexican, victim of the Capsaicin Withdrawal Blues.

No one of them would tell you he's aching for a taste of home and 8-Methyl-N-vanillyl-6-nonenamide — or even for a dash of capsaicin, the name given that unwieldly chemical designation. They would tell you, instead, that they have found not one, *not one* decent restaurant anywhere in town (this could be in a city of millions), that they can't find an enchilada anywhere, that if they ask for chile they get a red, soupy concoction of meat and something, that the best taco stand around offers Tabasco for a sauce. And it's chile they want — green chile, or red chile, but *chile*. The pod, not the soup. Chile with *flavor*, not just heat. New Mexico chile.

Capsaicin, or an isomer thereof, is that oily, orangish acid layered along the seeds and veins of the chile pod, one of New Mexico's officially adopted state symbols. Capsaicin, then, makes chile chile, gives it the piquancy ranging from innocuous to incendiary, brings tears to the eater's eyes, blisters to his lips, fire to his belly — and joy to his heart.

Chile: Spicy, flavorful, unique — indeed a symbol specific to the heart of the Southwest and a fitting catalyst for that ancient disease of the displaced.

Chile: Ancient, honored, symbolic. A spice — and a fruit unto itself. A demigod and a symbol, the center of controversy — of national combat.

Chile: More acres of it grow in New Mexico than all the other states put together.

Chile: Although New Mexicans consume more per capita than do any others of the United States and have adopted it as an official symbol, we are not the first to honor it. The Aztecs accorded chile the status of a minor god — a war god — and tempered adoration with fear of the flamboyant fire contained in our present crops' ancestors. Known to the Aztecs as *Chili* and *Axi* (*chile* is the Spanish — and favored — spelling in New Mexico), the chile and its ire were cooled by culinary marriage to *tomatl*, the tomato. It was a marriage of cousins, but one that worked to the advantage of each of these noble families. (Chile is also cousin to the potato, another New World gift, and to the eggplant. Green chile chopped into and fried with diced potatoes is a hearty breakfast side dish and another fine marriage of cousins. And green chile wed to the tomato and comforting the eggplant gives the eggplant parmesan a whole New World flavor.)

Popularity is, of course, reason enough for increasing demand, and along with interest shown by the *New York Times,* *Esquire* ran an interview with an anonymous (good thing for him) person who claimed to be creator of the world's greatest chile. With cheek, he promotes a concoction that combines, with twelve pounds of cubed brisket, as much oregano, and as much cumin, as chile powder — not to mention gobs, dashes and spoonfuls of cayenne, Dijon mustard, lime and lemon juice, sugar (sugar?), woodruff (woodruff??), garlic, gumbo file, chicken fat, beer, *and Tabasco and Worcestershire sauce, for crying out loud.* One wonders what color the mess might be.

Still, the word is spreading, and the International Connoisseurs of Green and Red Chile's membership list shows that it's not just the Spaniards' descendants who tang their tongues with New Mexico's best.

The chile didn't originate here (although its more sublime developments took place along the New Mexican Rio Grande); anthropologists digging in South America have dated plant remains to 700 B.C. Those pods must have been incredibly hot, if age is a yardstick and later Aztec crops were believed to be gods of war. But it is old even here; Spanish expeditions of the late 1500s reported New Mexico's Puebloans growing it and producing a (relatively) milder variant that could be eaten without addition of tomatoes — or eggplant. Very likely, the natives obtained it as an item of trade.

In modern times, the fame and success of New Mexico's co-state vegetable (the other being the pinto bean) may be due in large part to one man.

Dr. Roy Minoru Nakayama — who admits the chile is botanically a fruit, despite the New Mexico State Legislature's making it a vegetable — may well be the world's foremost authority on chiles. His doctoral dissertation was done on chile diseases.

An associate professor at New Mexico State University's agricultural research station, Dr. Nakayama comes by his interest naturally. He was born to it.

Son of a farmer in the village of Doña Ana, near Las Cruces, he — as do the sons of farmers everywhere — worked in the fields — including chile fields.

He thinks chile is better — certainly more popular — than it was when he picked it as a lad.

"The big difference, actually, way back then — even just prior to 1955 — was that about the only variety available here was a real hot chile. Too doggone hot for most," he says. "Most of it was the native chile, with some New Mexico No. 9. That No. 9 was larger-bodied, but it was too hot.

"We couldn't sell it outside the state."

A landmark year, 1955: New Mexico No. 6 came into production, a production that slowly increased as New Mexico farmers could sell their crop outside the state, catering to the milder tastes of Midwesterners.

Another landmark year, 1974: The Numex Big Jim goes into commercial production, end result of a decade's research and hybridization that saw Dr. Nakayama and associates borrow pollen from a tiny, Peruvian variety, cross it with Anaheim, native Chimayo and other New Mexican varieties, and plant, water, wait, weigh and taste. It takes anywhere from about seven to ten or more years before you get results.

The Numex Big Jim, named in honor of Dr. Nakayama's home state and Jim Lytle, a Las Cruces-area farmer who has worked closely in these experiments, produces pods about a foot long and weighing maybe three to the pound. It's bred so that the pods mature concurrently, making machine picking — and thus greater acreage — possible. Its size and weight surpassed other popular varieties. The heat of Numex Big Jim (rated on a scale that has Anaheim and New Mexico No. 6 as 1, Tabasco at 8), scales at 3.

Dr. Nakayama is modestly proud of his accomplishment.

"It has a different makeup from any other chile," he says.

As an authority on chile, Dr. Nakayama shows the usual embarrassment of a scientist confronted with an unscientific question.

"I haven't found any chile that's any better than what we have here. In fact, in some areas, frankly, I feel that some of the chiles just don't have the flavor of these grown in New Mexico."

He himself prefers milder chile, but is often called upon to judge in chile cookoffs and other such catastrophes. An ulcer, legacy of a German prisoner-of-war camp, must be placated with antacids before he renders taste and judgment.

4 "I used to like the real hot one, but it didn't quite agree with me," he confides. "So now I eat the milder ones — hot enough to let me know I'm eating chile."

The Nakayama Scale

How hot is hot? According to scientists, one part in one hundred thousand of the magic ingredient capsaicin can be detected by taste. Dr. Roy Nakayama, however, has a taste test scale that is geared for the layman. Keeping in mind that drought can increase the fire in any given crop, here is his scale, rising in heat from one to ten.

10. Bahamian
 9. Santaca (Japanese)
 8. Tabasco
 7. Jalapeño
 6. Española and Cayenne
 5. Sandia
 4. Hot Ancho
 3. Numex Big Jim
 2. Rio Grande
 1. New Mexico No. 6 and Anaheim

PREPARING
FRESH GREEN CHILE

First you catch your green chiles — perhaps from the Mesilla or Española valleys or the Chimayo area — and then follow this procedure (better wear rubber gloves):

Slit pods lengthwise and remove seeds and veins. Place pods on a cookie sheet under broiler. Or place on your outdoor grill. Allow pods to blister well on each side. Turn frequently so they don't burn. (Tongs would be handy for this.) Remove from fire and cover with damp towels for 10 to 15 minutes. Then peel skin from stem downward. Chiles are then ready to use or to freeze for the future.

6

FRESH RED CHILE

Fresh red chiles may be prepared the same way.

RISTRA SAUCE

Take chile pods from your Christmas ristra and wash well. You may toast these in a warm oven first, for a "brown" flavor —but don't let them burn. Remove seeds and veins. Pop them into the electric blender and grind to a powder. (If you don't mind the heat, leave the seeds in. But don't say we didn't warn you.) Now you have chile powder to use in chile sauce.

GREEN CHILE SAUCE

¼ cup salad or olive oil
1 clove garlic (optional)
½ cup minced onion (optional)
1 tablespoon flour
1 cup water
1 cup diced green chile
Salt to taste

Saute garlic and onion in heavy saucepan. Blend in flour with wooden spoon. Add water and green chile. Bring to a boil and simmer, stirring frequently, for 5 minutes.

RED CHILE SAUCE

3 tablespoons olive oil or lard
1 clove garlic, minced
2 tablespoons flour
½ cup chile powder
2 cups water
Salt to taste

Saute garlic in oil. Blend in flour with a wooden spoon. Add chile powder and blend in. (Don't let pan get too hot — chile will burn easily.) Blend in water and cook to desired consistency. Add salt to taste.

TAME GREEN CHILE SAUCE

1 cup mild diced green chile
4 cups cut up tomatoes and juice
2 tablespoons olive oil
1 clove garlic, minced
1 tablespoon flour
Salt to taste

Saute garlic in olive oil in heavy saucepan. Blend in flour. Add chile (fresh, canned or frozen) and tomatoes (fresh peeled or canned). Mix well and bring to boil. Simmer, stirring occasionally, for 5 to 10 minutes. Add more water if necessary.

If desired, ½ cup minced onion may be added with garlic and sauteed.

8

SALSA

2 tomatoes, medium size
1 Bermuda onion, medium size
1 clove garlic
½ teaspoon salt
2 or more green chiles

Use fresh chiles (roasted, peeled and seeded) or frozen or canned chiles. Chop the chiles, tomatoes and onion very fine. (Don't lose the juice of the tomatoes!) Mash the garlic with the salt. Mix well. Add more chiles to suit your taste. Allow flavors to blend at least an hour before using. Store in refrigerator or freezer. Use on tacos, eggs or hamburgers or as a dip for tostados. Makes about 1 pint.

BREADS

HOW TO BUILD AN HORNO— *An Outdoor Oven*

plans by Robert Montoya

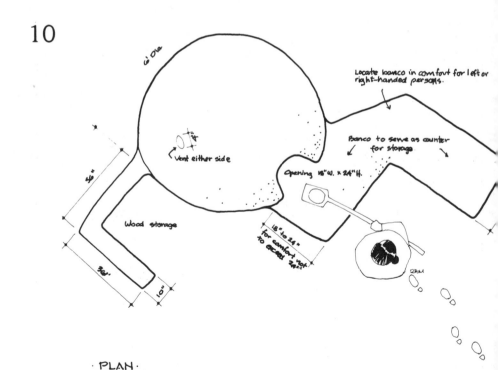

Locate banco in comfort for left or right-handed persons.

Banco to serve as counter for storage

Opening 18" W. x 24" H.

6' Dia.

Vent either side

Wood storage

18" to 24" for comfort "not to exceed 24"

4'0"

3'0"

10"

2 ball

· PLAN ·

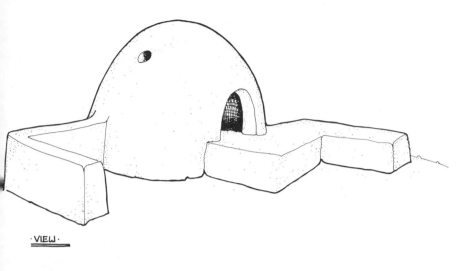

· VIEW ·

So you want to build an *horno* in your own backyard! Robert Montoya, an architect who is a San Juan-Sandia Pueblo Indian, has designed working plans for the readers of **New Mexico Magazine**. Bob's version, made with standard adobes, 10" x 14" x 4", has a round oven base and an elongated "lip" to use as a work surface. He has also included a short wall.

"A left-handed cook might want this plan reversed," Bob suggests.

Adobes are available in many parts of the country. But where they cannot be obtained, the home builder may wish to adapt the plans to brick, lining the firebox with firebrick.

In areas where rain is likely to be a problem, the adobe oven should be covered with a cement stucco, as indicated in Bob's plans.

A door, cut from metal or plywood, is handy to lean against the oven opening to retain the heat. And a flat wooden paddle, not unlike a narrow snow shovel, is used for sliding the pots and pans into, and out of, the oven.

Once you have built your horno, you have to learn how to heat and use this unusual and useful outdoor oven. The first step is to collect firewood and build a fire inside the oven. Small branches are better than big logs, and juniper is a favorite wood among New Mexicans.

When the roaring fire has died down to coals, the ashes must be swept out the front of the oven. This is done by using a pole with a towel tied to the end of it. Dip the towel in a pail of water, and swab out the oven floor. A broom helps remove the ashes, too. But be careful not to set the broom on fire!

Next comes the temperature-taking. Toss a crumpled sheet of newspaper into the oven. If the newspaper burns right up

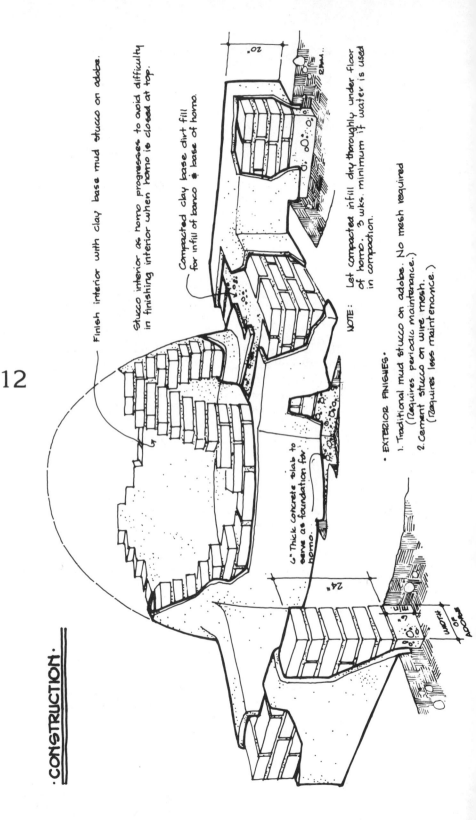

· CONSTRUCTION·

12

Finish interior with clay base mud stucco on adobe.

Stucco interior as horno progresses to avoid difficulty in finishing interior when horno is closed at top.

Compacted clay base dirt fill for infill of banco & base of horno.

6" Thick concrete slab to serve as foundation for horno.

20"

24"

24"MIN.

3"E

WIDTH OF ADOBE

NOTE: Let compacted infill dry thoroughly under floor of horno. 3 wks. minimum if water is used in compaction.

· EXTERIOR FINISHES·

1. Traditional mud stucco on adobe. No mesh required
   (Requires periodic maintenance.)

2. Cement stucco on wire mesh.
   (Requires less maintenance.)

the oven is too hot. Swab it out with more cold water. When the temperature is right for bread — medium hot — the sheet of newspaper will brown slowly, like a piece of toast. When you use an outdoor oven regularly, you soon learn to judge its temperature within a few degrees. (Some New Mexicans judge the temperature by tossing in a handful of oatmeal.)

If the oven seems a little hot for the dishes you are baking, leave the door uncovered. Otherwise, place a piece of wood over the opening to retain the heat.

An oven like this should bake 25 to 50 loaves of bread at once, followed by cakes, cookies, pies and puddings, and perhaps the holiday turkeys overnight.

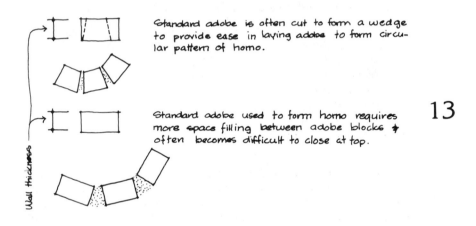

Standard adobe is often cut to form a wedge to provide ease in laying adobe to form circular pattern of horno.

Standard adobe used to form horno requires more space filling between adobe blocks & often becomes difficult to close at top.

13

ROSELLA'S FAMOUS BREAD

Rosella Frederick of Cochiti Pueblo has graciously shared her bread recipe with **New Mexico Magazine.** And, yes, those measurements are correct. She uses just one envelope of dry yeast to make 25 loaves of bread. The long rising period makes a fine-textured bread. At altitudes below 6,000 feet you might want to increase the rising time of the dough, or, if you prefer, use 2 envelopes of dry yeast.

25 pounds unbleached flour
2 cups lard
3 tablespoons salt
1 envelope dry yeast
3 cups warm water
1 teaspoon sugar
8 quarts warm water

14

Mix flour, salt and lard together, working in lard until it is finely crumbled. Dissolve yeast and sugar in 3 cups of warm water. Mix into flour mixture along with 8 quarts of lukewarm water. Mix well until dough becomes elastic. This is a job that takes strong arms! Cover and let rise in a warm part of the kitchen for about 8 hours. During that time, punch the dough down twice. After it has risen the third time, form into round loaves. (Rosella cuts some of hers into fancy shapes.) Place loaves in pie pans. Rub tops with softened lard. Cover and let rise again for about a half hour. (During this time, Rosella prepares the fire in her *horno* — the outdoor oven.) Bake for 45 minutes to 1 hour in moderately hot oven. Makes 15-25 loaves, depending on size.

PAN DE LA REINA

Alicia Romero contributed this delicious holiday bread recipe to **New Mexico Magazine** many years ago.

1 *envelope yeast*
½ *cup warm water*
1 *teaspoon sugar*
4 *cups flour*
1 *cup butter or margarine*
½ *teaspoon salt*
2 *tablespoons sugar*
6 *eggs, beaten*
1 *cup milk*
1 *teaspoon anise seeds*

15

Dissolve the yeast in warm water. Mix in 1 teaspoon sugar and just enough flour to make a soft ball. Cover and place in a warm place to rise for at least an hour. Add the remaining flour, melted butter, salt, sugar, eggs, milk and anise seeds and mix and knead until smooth and velvety. Cover and let rise to double its original bulk. Punch down and knead slightly. Pull off small pieces, mold into balls and place in a greased tube pan. Cover and set in warm place and let rise until double in size. Bake at 350 degrees F until it is brown and shining. Rub the surface with melted butter.

SOPAIPILLAS

Although they are kin to fry bread and cousin to buñelos, New Mexico's sopaipillas are unique. There's nothing in the world quite like these light crispy bread puffs.

2 cups flour
2 teaspoons baking powder
1 teaspoon salt
2 tablespoons lard
½ cup water
Shortening for frying

16 Sift dry ingredients together. Work in lard and lukewarm water to make a soft dough. Chill in refrigerator. Roll out dough on a floured surface to about ¼-inch thickness. Cut into 3-inch squares. Deep fry in hot lard (or vegetable shortening) at 400 degrees F a few at a time. Brown on each side and drain on paper towels. Serve piping hot. To eat, poke open and pour in honey or slather with honey butter.

HONEY BUTTER

Cream 1 cup butter or margarine. Gradually beat in ½ cup to 1 cup of honey.* Cover and store in refrigerator. Serve with sopaipillas. Good also on hot biscuits or toast.

*If your honey has begun to crystalize, you can use the larger amount.

FLOUR TORTILLAS

2 cups flour
1 teaspoon salt
½ teaspoon baking powder
3 tablespoons lard
½ cup warm water

Mix the flour, salt and baking powder. Work in lard. Add water and mix well. Knead dough until it feels elastic. Cover and let stand for 20 to 30 minutes. Pinch off pieces of dough about the size of an egg. Roll into a ball in your hands. Then roll out on a lightly floured board to about 6 or 7 inches in diameter. Bake on a hot, ungreased griddle until lightly browned on each side. They should still be soft and supple. Cover with a clean towel to keep warm and soft until serving. Or store in a plastic bag in the freezer. Makes about 10 tortillas.

QUICKIE TORTILLAS

Angie M. Garcia recommends this as a quick and easy method of making flour tortillas.

1 tube refrigerator biscuits
Flour

Use plain or buttermilk biscuits. On a floured surface, pat out each biscuit to desired thickness — ⅛ to ¼ inch. Place each tortilla on a hot griddle (475 to 500 degrees F) and cook for about 2 minutes. Turn and cook on the other side until done. Makes 10.

QUICK NAVAJO TORTILLAS

3 cups flour
1 ½ teaspoons baking powder
½ teaspoon salt
1 ⅓ cups warm water

Mix flour, baking powder and salt. Add 1 cup of the water and mix, adding more water as needed to make dough soft but not sticky. Knead smooth. Tear off a chunk about the size of a small peach. Roll in a ball then flatten out to about 1/8 inch. Place on a grate over a glowing fire and bake until brown. Turn and cook on other side. Serve with butter and honey or use as bread with Navajo mutton stew. They may also be baked on your pancake griddle at home.

18

NAVAJO FRY BREAD

3 cups flour
1 ½ teaspoons baking powder
½ teaspoon salt
1 ⅓ cups warm water
Shortening

Use either all white or half whole wheat flour. Mix flour, baking powder and salt. Add warm water and mix. Dough should be soft but not sticky. Knead until smooth. Tear off a chunk about the size of a peach. Pat and stretch until it is thin. Poke a hole through the middle, and drop into sizzling hot deep fat. (Lard is the traditional shortening, but you might prefer to use vegetable oil.) Brown on both sides. Drain and serve hot. Eat with honey or jam.

INDIAN FRY BREAD

This version doesn't use baking powder, which can be in short supply on the remote reaches of the reservation.

2 cups flour
4 tablespoons powdered milk
1 teaspoon salt
Lukewarm water
Shortening

Combine flour, milk and salt. Add enough lukewarm water to make a soft dough. Divide dough in half and pat out until it is about ¼ inch thick. Fry in large frying pan in about an inch of hot lard (or vegetable shortening). Brown on both sides. Drain. Serve hot with honey or jelly.

19

SOURDOUGH

When the West was young, no kitchen, no chuckwagon was without its crock of "starter" — wild yeast, fermenting and bubbling, which had to be fed with fresh batter each time some of it was used. Kept warm during frigid winters — sometimes tucked into the cook's bedroll — some starters are reputed to have lasted more than a hundred years. A cup of starter, a spoonful of "sody" and the makings of great biscuits, bread or flapjacks were well begun.

20

SOURDOUGH STARTER #1

2 cups flour
2 cups warm water *
1 teaspoon salt

Mix together in glass or china bowl. Let stand, covered, in a warm place for 2 to 4 days, until sour and bubbly.

SOURDOUGH STARTER #2

2 cups flour
2 cups lukewarm water *
1 tablespoon sugar
1 envelope dry yeast

In a nonmetallic container, mix all ingredients to a smooth paste. Cover and set in a warm place for 2 to 3 days, stirring occasionally. The starter will be thick.

*Or do what the old-timers did, and use the water in which you boiled your potatoes.

SOURDOUGH BISCUITS

1   cup sourdough starter
3-4 cups flour
1   teaspoon salt
1   teaspoon sugar
1   teaspoon baking soda
1   tablespoon melted shortening

Place 3 cups flour in a bowl and add sourdough starter. Stir in salt, soda and sugar. Add shortening. Gradually mix in enough additional flour to make a stiff dough. Add enough cooking oil to the bottom of a medium size dutch oven to just cover the bottom. Pinch off dough about the size of a large walnut. Form into a ball and roll it in the shortening in the dutch oven. Repeat until biscuits are crowded together in the oven. Cover and allow to rise in a warm place about 45 minutes. Then bake for 15 minutes in hot oven (400 degrees F). Or, set oven into hot coals of a campfire, cover lid with hot coals and bake for 15 minutes.

SOURDOUGH FLAPJACKS

½ cup sourdough starter
2 eggs
2 tablespoons syrup
¼ cup oil
1 cup milk
2 cups flour
½ teaspoon salt
1 teaspoon baking soda

Beat all the ingredients together lightly with a fork. If mixture seems too thick, add more milk. Bake on a hot griddle, preferably in the wilderness.

23

OLD-TIME BATTER BISCUITS

1   envelope dried yeast
¼   cup warm water
1   cup milk
½   cup butter
3   tablespoons sugar or honey
1 ½ teaspoons salt
1   egg, beaten
3 ½ cups flour

24

Dissolve the yeast in warm water. Scald the milk and drop in the butter, sugar or honey, and salt. Stir until dissolved. Cool to lukewarm, then mix in the yeast and egg. Beat in the flour. Cover and allow to rise in a warm place until it is double. Stir down. Spoon into well-greased muffin tins, filling no more than half full. Allow to rise to the tops of the pans. Then bake at 375 degrees F until they are brown.

FRONTIER DOUGHNUTS

These doughnuts may be made at home — or over the camp-fire.

6¾ cups flour
10   teaspoons baking powder
1   teaspoon salt
2⅔ cups sugar
2   teaspoons nutmeg
4   eggs, beaten
2½ cups milk
2   teaspoons oil or melted shortening

Shortening for frying
1   cup sugar
2   teaspoons cinnamon
½   teaspoon nutmeg

Mix all ingredients together until blended. Roll out about a half inch thick on a floured surface. Cut with a doughnut cutter. Deep fry in melted shortening or salad oil (a dutch oven is ideal) over medium flame. (Shortening should be around 365 degrees F.) Turn to brown on each side. Drain doughnuts on paper towels, then drop into a paper bag containing sugar, cinnamon and nutmeg, and shake. Makes 96.

DON'S CORNBREAD

From *Pearl's Dining Room* in Lovington comes this good basic cornbread recipe.

1½ cups buttermilk
1   teaspoon salt
2   cups cornmeal
1   cup flour
2   tablespoons baking powder
¼   cup sugar
2   eggs
⅓   cup melted butter or margarine

26   Mix all ingredients together with a fork. Don't overmix. Turn into a buttered 9 x 9 pan. Bake at 425 degrees F until golden brown — about 20 minutes. Cut in squares and serve hot.

NEW MEXICO SPOON BREAD

It's hard to beat this recipe developed by New Mexico State University. It's from their Cooperative Extension Service Circular 396, entitled "Chile."

1 #300 can cream-style corn
¾ cup milk
⅓ cup melted shortening
1 ½ cups cornmeal
2 eggs, slightly beaten
½ teaspoon soda
1 teaspoon baking powder
1 teaspoon salt
1 teaspoon sugar (optional)
1 4-ounce can chopped green chile
1 ½ cups grated cheddar cheese

Mix all ingredients except chile and cheese. Pour half the batter in greased 9 x 9 pan, sprinkle with half the cheese and chile. Add remaining batter and top with cheese and chile. Bake at 400 degrees F for 45 minutes. We think a little minced onion added to the batter would be good, too.

PEANUT CORN PATTY CAKES

Carolyn Durrett dreamed up this prizewinner.

1 cup cornmeal
1 teaspoon baking powder
¾ teaspoon salt
1 cup cream-style canned corn
¼ cup milk
1 egg
⅓ cup chopped salted peanuts

Sift together cornmeal, baking powder and salt into a bowl. Add remaining ingredients and stir until all dry ingredients have been moistened. Drop by large spoonfuls onto a hot greased griddle. Bake until browned on one side, then turn and brown on the other side. Serve hot with butter and syrup.

SAN JUAN HUSH PUPPIES

¾ cup cornmeal
¼ cup flour
3 teaspoons baking powder
½ teaspoon garlic salt
1 egg
½ cup milk
1 small onion, minced
½ cup chopped green chile
Shortening

Mix cornmeal, flour, baking powder and garlic salt together. Beat in egg and milk with a fork. Mix in onion and green chile (canned, fresh or frozen). Drop by tablespoon into hot fat. Brown on one side, turn, and brown on the other. Makes about 20 pups. Serve with fish.

BLUE CORN BREAD

From the northern part of the Navajo Reservation comes this unusual recipe. Obviously the recipe is not for the average American kitchen. But it shows the remarkable ingenuity of people who must use the ingredients available far from supermarkets.

1 cup cedar ashes
1 cup hot water
1 pound blue cornmeal
1 quart water

The cedar ashes (really from juniper wood, locally called cedar) should be smooth and fine. Sieve if possible. Mix the ashes with hot water and remove any twigs or other bits of rough material. Add to blue cornmeal. Pour in water gradually, adding only enough to make a soft dough. Form into cakes about a half inch thick. Smooth the surface of the cakes with water. Cook on a medium hot grill on each side until the cakes are done. Use like bread.

PECAN WAFFLES

3 eggs
¼ cup cooking oil
1 cup yogurt
1 ½ cups pancake mix
½ cup chopped New Mexico pecans

Beat eggs, add oil, mix in yogurt. Add mixture slowly to pancake mix, beating with a fork until well blended. If yogurt is very thick, add a little milk to batter. Fold in pecans. Bake in a hot waffle iron. Serve immediately with butter, syrup, honey or honey butter. Serves 3. Keep batter in refrigerator while first batch is baking.

30 Leftover waffles may be frozen and heated up later in a toaster. But be careful — they burn very easily.

VEGETABLES, SALADS AND SIDE DISHES

GUACAMOLE LA TERTULIA

Every week, visitors to *La Tertulia* in Santa Fe plead for the "secret" guacamole recipe. And June Ortiz hesitates. "I'm really embarrassed to give it to them because it's so simple," she confesses.

1 ripe avocado
¼ teaspoon garlic salt
Lettuce
Tostadas or corn chips

Peel and mash the ripe avocado. Mix in the garlic salt. Serve on lettuce with crisp tostadas or corn chips. Serves 2.

32

BILL'S GUACAMOLE

6-8 ripe avocados
¼   cup finely chopped onion
1   large tomato, diced
½   cup chopped green chile
2-3 minced jalapeño peppers
1   clove garlic, minced
Dash of cumin powder
1   teaspoon lemon juice
Salt to taste

Peel and pit avocados. Mash coarsely with a fork, leaving bits of whole avocado. Stir in remaining ingredients. Serve on lettuce or as a dip with tostados.

CHUNKY GUACAMOLE

1 large ripe avocado
1 medium tomato
1 small onion
1 small bell pepper
3 long green chiles
Juice of ½ lemon
Salt to taste

Chop all the ingredients fine. Do not mash. Use fresh roasted and peeled chiles, but, if they are not available, use canned or frozen. Mix together with the lemon juice and add salt to taste. Serve as a dip or as a salad with lettuce and corn chips.

33

WALDORF SALAD, NEW MEXICO

1 cup diced unpeeled New Mexico apples
1 teaspoon lemon juice
½ cup coarsely chopped New Mexico pecans
½ cup diced celery
¼ cup mayonnaise
   or mayonnaise and yogurt mixed

Mix lemon juice into apples. Mix in remaining ingredients.
Chill. Serve on lettuce. Serves 3 to 4.

34

SALAD ROMANO

An unusual "white" salad, this is served at *Casa Vieja* in
Corrales.

2 cups sliced fresh white mushrooms
2 cups inner stalks of celery, thinly sliced crosswise
2 cups coarsely grated imported Swiss cheese
Vinaigrette dressing
Coarse salt
Pepper

Mushrooms should be very fresh and very thinly sliced. Toss
ingredients with dressing. Serve with coarse salt and freshly
ground pepper. Serves 4 to 6.

BLUE CHEESE DRESSING

The dining room of the old *Eklund Hotel* in Clayton has become a regular stop for travelers in northeastern New Mexico. This is the recipe for their special blue cheese dressing.

⅔ cup blue cheese
⅓ cup mayonnaise
1 tablespoon sauterne
½ teaspoon sugar
⅓ tablespoon Worcestershire sauce

Crumble cheese. Stir in small amount of mayonnaise. Add remaining ingredients except for mayonnaise, which can be gradually added to taste and desired consistency. Stir and stir until only small chunks remain. The ingredients may be altered to suit individual taste.

35

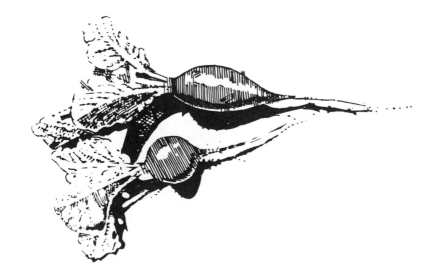

PINTO SALAD

The Public Service Company of New Mexico suggests this for a patio supper.

2½ cups cooked pinto beans
6   hard-cooked eggs, chopped
1   cup cubed longhorn cheese
¼   cup thin onion rings
2   tablespoons salad dressing
1   tablespoon chile sauce
1   teaspoon prepared mustard
¼   cup bacon bits
Salt and pepper to taste

36

Combine beans, eggs, cheese and onion. Chill. When ready to serve, mix salad dressing, chile sauce, mustard, salt and pepper together and toss with bean mixture. Sprinkle with bacon bits. Serves 6 to 8.

3-BEAN SALAD

1   17-ounce can green beans
1   15-ounce can garbanzos
1   16-ounce can red kidney beans
1   green pepper
1   red onion
¼   teaspoon garlic salt
½   cup oil and vinegar dressing

Drain beans well. Slice pepper and onion into thin slivers. Toss beans, onions, pepper and garlic salt gently with dressing. Chill well and serve. Serves 6 to 8.

QUELITES

If you have access to wild spinach, that's really what you should use in this recipe. But most people make do with the "tame" kind.

½ pound fresh spinach
    or 1 10-ounce package frozen spinach
1 tablespoon shortening
3 tablespoons chopped onion
¼ teaspoon crushed red chile
Salt to taste

Wash spinach well, chop and steam about 10 minutes or until tender. Saute the onion in shortening, mix in drained spinach, chile and salt, and cook for an additional 5 minutes. Serves 2 to 3.

37

FRIED SQUASH BLOSSOMS

An old custom — collecting the "male" blossoms.

12 large squash blossoms
¼ teaspoon ground cumin
¼ teaspoon garlic salt
½ cup flour
½ teaspoon baking powder
1 egg
½ cup milk
1 tablespoon salad oil
Oil for frying

38 Wash blossoms, dry on paper towels. Sift dry ingredients together. Beat egg in milk and salad oil. Gradually mix into dry ingredients. Dip blossoms in batter. Fry a few at a time in deep fat fryer at 375 degrees F until crisp. Or fry in 2 inches hot oil in heavy frying pan, turning to brown evenly. Drain on paper towels. Serves 4.

ZUCCHINI WITH GARLIC

4-6 zucchini
1   clove garlic
1   teaspoon salt
¼   cup oil or lard
Pepper

Wash zucchini and split lengthwise. Mash garlic clove in salt. (Or use garlic salt instead.) Rub salt on cut sides of zucchini. Saute in medium hot oil or lard — but not too hot or the squash will burn. When they are brown, turn them carefully and cook on the other side. Sprinkle with pepper and serve. Serves 4.

39

CALABACITAS

This is one of the most popular vegetable dishes in New Mexico and deserves to be better known in the rest of the country. It's delicious!

2   tablespoons oil or lard
1   clove garlic
1   medium onion
4   medium large zucchini
1   12-ounce can niblet corn, drained
1   4-ounce can diced green chiles
*   or 2 fresh peeled chiles*
Salt to taste
½ cup grated cheddar, jack or longhorn cheese

In a large heavy skillet, saute the onion, garlic and zuccini in oil. Discard the garlic. Mix in drained corn, chopped chiles and salt. Cover tightly and heat through. Mix in cheese and serve. Serves 4.

40

BAKED INDIAN PUMPKIN

When they are using the outdoor oven — the *horno* — Hispanic and Indian cooks don't like to waste the heat. When they have finished baking bread and pies, they often will cook items that require a less hot oven. Pumpkins, for instance.

Clean whole pumpkins well. Remove the tops, as if you were going to make jack-o-lanterns. Scoop out seeds and fibers. Place pumpkins in warm oven. Cover the oven opening. Leave the pumpkins overnight. To serve, cut in wedges, sprinkle with sugar or cinnamon sugar, pour on cream — and eat. Or serve with salt, pepper and butter. Or scoop out cooked contents to use for pumpkin pie. The pumpkin pulp can be frozen for future use. Of course, you can bake a pumpkin in your own kitchen stove, too. Preheat your oven to 350 degrees F. Place the prepared pumpkin on a pan in the oven. Reduce heat to 225 degrees F and bake for 4 or 5 hours for a medium pumpkin.

BAKED SQUASH

1 small acorn or Hubbard squash
Salt and pepper
2 tablespoons melted butter
2 teaspoons brown sugar
2 teaspoons rum

Cut squash in half. Remove seeds. Sprinkle with salt and pepper. Brush with butter, sprinkle with sugar and rum. Place in baking dish. Cover with foil. Bake at 375 degrees F until tender — about an hour. Serves 2.

COLACHE

¼ cup oil or lard
4 cups diced pumpkin or acorn squash
1 onion, chopped
1 clove garlic, minced
1 green pepper, chopped
1 green or red chile, chopped
1 14-ounce can stewed tomatoes
  or 4 tomatoes
1 12-ounce can niblet corn, drained
Salt to taste

Saute squash or pumpkin in oil in large heavy skillet for 5 minutes. Mix in remaining ingredients. Cover and simmer gently until cooked — about 15 to 20 minutes. Add water if necessary. Serves 8.

BERENJENA Y CHILE VERDE

New Mexico State University's Cooperative Extension Service developed this tasty combination of eggplant and green chile.

1 large eggplant
1 egg
2 cups soft breadcrumbs
6 strips bacon
1 small onion, diced
1 cup green chile, chopped
Salt

42

Peel eggplant, cut in cubes and cook in slightly salted water until tender. Drain and cool. Combine onion, well-beaten egg, chile, breadcrumbs, salt. Mix with eggplant. Put in buttered casserole. Top with bacon strips. Bake uncovered in moderate (350-degree F) oven for about 45 minutes. Serves 5 to 6.

CHILE PANCAKES

Maybe this recipe isn't traditional, but its flavors are. Serve as a side dish for dinner — or for an eye-opening breakfast.

3 eggs, separated
2 tablespoons flour
1 teaspoon minced onion
Dash Worcestershire sauce
1 4-ounce can diced green chiles
Salt to taste

Beat egg whites stiff but not dry. Beat egg yolks until thick, then beat in flour. Mix in onion, chiles, Worcestershire sauce and salt. Fold in egg whites. Spoon onto a moderately hot greased griddle and brown on both sides. Serves 4.

CATTLE KING POTATOES

3 pounds potatoes
1 clove garlic
Salt
⅓ cup butter
2 egg yolks
½ cup cream
½ pound mushrooms
¼ cup minced parsley
Pepper

Peel potatoes, cut in uniform size, boil with garlic and salt until tender. Meanwhile, slice and saute the mushrooms in 1 tablespoon of the butter. Mash potatoes with remaining butter. Beat egg yolks with cream and mix into the potatoes along with the mushrooms and parsley. Add more salt if necessary and pepper to taste. Pile in a buttered baking dish and bake at 375 degrees F until brown. Serves 8 to 10.

SPANISH RICE

¼ cup olive oil
1 onion
½ bell pepper
1 clove garlic
1 14-ounce can stewed tomatoes
1 teaspoon chile powder
Dash Worcestershire sauce
1 cup rice
2 cups water
Salt and pepper to taste

44

Chop onion and pepper and mince garlic. Saute in olive oil until onion is transparent. Mix in remaining ingredients. Bring to a boil and simmer, tightly covered, on lowest heat for about 20 minutes. Stir occasionally. Serves 4 to 6.

FRIJOLES

This is the basic bean recipe.

3 cups pinto beans
4 quarts water
1 clove garlic
1 cup diced salt pork
Salt

Wash beans well, cover with water and soak overnight. Drain.
Put beans, water, garlic and salt pork — but not salt — in a
large heavy kettle. Cover tightly, bring to a boil, and simmer
for about 1½ hours or until the beans are tender but not
mushy. Add boiling water during the cooking if necessary and
stir occasionally. When the beans are done, remove lid, turn up
heat and cook until all liquid has been absorbed. Add salt to
taste.

FRIJOLES REFRITOS

Mash leftover beans and fry in bacon fat until hot. Sprinkle
with grated cheddar or longhorn cheese. Serve.

Use refried beans as a filling for tacos and burritos.

LINCOLN COUNTY PUDDING

When in New Mexico . . . Some British immigrants looked at their Yorkshire pudding recipes, looked at the materials on hand, and came up with this zingy version of an old favorite.

Pan drippings from roasted meat
3 eggs
¾ cup flour
2 tablespoons red chile powder
¼ teaspoon ground cumin
1 cup milk
½ teaspoon salt
1 tablespoon minced onion

46

Set your roast — beef, turkey, lamb, venison — aside in a warm place. Turn the oven up to 450 degrees F. Leave about ½ cup of drippings in the baking pan. Mix flour, salt, chile powder and cumin together. Beat eggs, milk and onion together, then beat in flour mixture. Turn into the hot drippings and bake for about 30 minutes. It should puff up and brown. Cut in squares and serve immediately with your roast.

MAIN DISHES

BREAKFAST TROUT

Let's say you've been fishing in the Gila high country or along the San Juan River and you've snagged your breakfast. Here's the next step.

Fry up a pound of thick-sliced bacon and set it aside to drain on paper towels or brown paper bags. Clean the trout well, using as little water as possible. Dry thoroughly. Roll in cornmeal. Fry the trout in the hot bacon fat. If you use the Canadian method, you'll allow 10 minutes per inch of thickness of the fish at its thickest point. It should be a nice golden brown. Don't overcook it and let it get dry. Allow 1 or 2 trout per person. Don't salt while they are cooking. The bacon fat may be salty enough. If you have the ingredients and the time, the perfect accompaniment to the trout would be New Mexico hush puppies. See page 28.

AUNT MARIKA'S STUFFED TROUT

On the other hand, let's suppose you have captured one of those Big Ones — the one that didn't get away. This is dinner fare, either in the outdoors or at home. Clean the fish well and keep it dry and cold until you're ready to use it. (Rolled in cornmeal, protected in a plastic bag, kept on ice.) Here are a couple of ways you might like to try your proud beauty.

1 3-5 pound trout
3 tablespoons butter
3 tablespoons chopped, toasted almonds
2 tablespoons minced onion
2 tablespoons minced parsley
½ teaspoon salt
Pepper
2 cups dry bread cubes
¼ cup minced dill pickle
Oil or melted butter

Melt 3 tablespoons butter in heavy pan. Stir in almonds, onion and parsley, and saute lightly. Mix in salt, pepper to taste, and bread cubes. Stir well. Last, mix in the dill pickle. Set fish on its back, belly side up, on a sheet of heavy-duty aluminum foil that has been rubbed with oil or melted butter. Brush sides of fish with oil or butter. Fill the cavity with stuffing. Fold the foil up to enclose the fish like a kayak, with a slight opening at top for breathing. Bake on a grill 6 inches over hot coals (or in a 425-degree F oven) for about a half hour if the fish is about 3 inches thick. Don't turn the fish on its sides. If necessary, wedge it with small rocks or set it in a cradle made with a bent wire coat hanger, to keep it on its back. One of the San Juan biggies stuffed this way should serve 3 or 4 persons — or 2 greedy ones.

POACHED TROUT

1 3-pound trout
4 tablespoons butter
3 slices tomato
3 slivers green pepper
½ cup sliced mushrooms
½ cup dry white wine
Salt and pepper

Lay the trout on a sheet of heavy-duty foil. Fold up sides to make a bed. Tuck 2 tablespoons of butter, a few of the sliced mushrooms and a sprinkle of salt and pepper inside the cavity. Arrange remaining mushrooms, slices of tomato, slivers of green pepper on top of fish. Pour wine gently over the fish. Dot top of fish with butter and sprinkle with salt and pepper. Fold foil over in a drugstore fold and seal package. Poke fork holes in top to allow steam to escape. Bury the package in coals and bake for 20 to 30 minutes, depending on how hot the coals seem and how thick the fish is. (10 minutes per inch of thickness.) This may serve 2 or 3 persons — then again it may not. It depends on how hungry the diners are and what else there is to eat.

HUEVOS RANCHEROS

Everyone has a special way of preparing huevos rancheros. This suggestion comes from New Mexico State University.

2 cups green or red chile sauce
4 eggs
½ cup grated cheese

Heat chile sauce in shallow frying pan. When hot, slip eggs into sauce from small dish or saucer, being careful not to break yolks. Cover and simmer over very low heat until eggs are poached to desired firmness. Serve on warm plates with remaining sauce poured over eggs. Sprinkle with cheese. Serves 2. Use canned sauce or your own mixture. For recipes, see page 7.

51

ANNE'S QUICHE

Anne Davenport's quiches have become legendary in the Santa Fe area and have been widely copied. Little wonder! Anne takes a basic quiche recipe made with cream — like the one below — and orchestrates her own delectable variations.

1   deep 9- or 10-inch pastry shell
1   egg white
1   cup finely minced ham
1 ½ cups grated Swiss cheese
2   eggs
2   egg yolks
1 ½ cups scalded cream
½   teaspoon salt
Pepper to taste
1   cup fresh sweet corn kernels (optional)
1   4-ounce can chopped green chile
    or ½ cup chopped fresh green chile
½   cup minced green onions

Brush the pastry shell with beaten egg white. Bake at 425 degrees F until the crust is set but not brown. Spread the minced cooked ham over the bottom. Sprinkle with the cheese. Beat the eggs and egg yolks with the scalded cream. Add salt, and pepper to taste. Slice the corn kernels from the cob with a sharp knife and remove any bits of corn silk. Add with the chopped green chile and minced green onions. Pour this mixture over the cheese and bake at 350 degrees F until the custard has set. This could also be baked in two 7- or 8-inch crusts. Or it could be baked in a 9-inch square baking dish and cut in squares to serve at a cocktail party.

QUICHE LORRAINE FARIGOULE

8- or 9-inch pastry shell, baked
2   strips bacon
2   tablespoons minced onion
¼   cup chopped ham
3-4 thin slices Swiss cheese
4   eggs, beaten
2   cups half-and-half
1   cup whipping cream
⅛   teaspoon salt
⅛   teaspoon nutmeg
Pinch of white pepper

Fry bacon, and when almost done, add chopped onion and fry together until bacon is done. Drain well. Crumble bacon into bottom of pie shell. Spread onions and ham in bottom of shell. Then cover with slices of Swiss cheese. To beaten eggs add half-and-half, whipping cream, salt, nutmeg and pepper. Blend well. Pour over cheese in pie shell. Bake at about 375° F for about 20 minutes. A knife plunged into the center should come out clean and top of quiche should be brown and puffy. Serves 4 to 6.

53

CHILE PIE

Not really a "pie," this is more like a quiche without a crust. Delectable as a main dish for lunch, it could also make a light supper. And how about doubling the recipe, making it in a rectangular baking dish, and cutting in small squares to serve at a party?

4-6 whole green chiles
1   cup grated jack or longhorn cheese
4   eggs
1   cup scalded half-and-half
*   or 1 cup evaporated milk*
½   teaspoon garlic salt

Line a buttered 8- or 9-inch pie pan with chiles (fresh, canned or frozen). Sprinkle with the cheese. Beat eggs and combine with half-and-half and garlic salt. Pour over cheese. Bake at 325 degrees F for about 40 minutes or until the custard has set. Cut in wedges and serve. Serves 4.

GREEN CHILE SOUFFLE

This happy marriage of green chile to a souffle was engineered by Edna Turner of Santa Fe.

5 egg whites
2 tablespoons grated Parmesan cheese
3 tablespoons butter
3 tablespoons flour
1 cup hot milk
½ teaspoon salt
¼ teaspoon dry mustard
Dash cayenne
¼ teaspoon Worcestershire sauce
4 egg yolks
Pinch salt
1 cup shredded sharp cheddar cheese
¼ to ½ cup chopped green chile

Place egg whites in a 4-quart bowl and let stand at room temperature 1 hour. Heat oven to 400 degrees F. Butter 1½-quart souffle dish generously. Sprinkle bottom and sides evenly with Parmesan cheese. Melt 3 tablespoons butter over low heat in heavy saucepan. Add flour and stir with wire whisk. Cook over low heat, stirring constantly until mixture foams and bubbles. Remove from heat, add milk, and beat until smooth. Beat in salt, mustard, cayenne and Worcestershire. Return to heat and cook 1 minute, stirring constantly, until mixture is quite thick. Remove from heat and add egg yolks 1 at a time, beating well after each addition. Pour this mixture into a large bowl. Beat egg whites with a pinch of salt until stiff peaks form. Add 1 large spoonful to the egg yolk mixture and blend. Add all but 1 tablespoon of the cheese and the chopped chiles (frozen, fresh or canned) to the egg yolk mixture and blend well. Spoon remaining egg whites on top and fold in with a rubber spatula. Pour into souffle dish and smooth with spatula. Sprinkle remaining cheese on top. Run a silver knife in a circle about 1 inch from the edge of dish. (This will enable the crown or "hat" to form when done.) Place in center of oven and reduce to 375 degrees F. Bake 34-40 minutes, or until knife inserted in the side comes out clean. Serve immediately.

PIÑON-RICE STUFFING

For your New Mexico turkey . . .

½ cup butter or margarine
½ cup green onions, chopped
½ cup minced parsley
1 cup piñon nuts
6 cups cooked rice
Salt and pepper to taste

Saute the onions in the butter. Mix all remaining ingredients, adding enough salt and pepper to taste. Stuff your turkey and roast as usual.

PIÑON TURKEY STUFFING

Marian Meyer, our piñon expert, suggests this elegant way of stuffing a turkey.

12 cups dry bread cubes
⅓ cup chopped parsley
¼ cup grated onion
2 teaspoons poultry seasoning
1 teaspoon salt
½ cup shelled piñon nuts
1 cup turkey or chicken broth

Combine all ingredients except broth. Add broth and toss lightly until moistened. Makes 8 cups or enough stuffing for a 12-pound turkey. (Note: In order not to overpower the delicate flavor of the piñon, seasonings are used with a light touch. Butter is not used because of the richness of the nuts.)

ENCHILADA PANCHO VILLA

The *Holiday Inn de Las Cruces* has come up with an enchilada recipe that is as unusual as it is tasty. The recipe brings thoughts of Vera Cruz rather than Las Cruces.

1 tablespoon butter
4 ounces crabmeat
1 flour tortilla
½ cup tomatillo sauce
2 tablespoons guacamole
¼ cup sour cream

Saute crabmeat in butter for 5 minutes. Warm tortilla on grill. Place crabmeat in center and roll up tortilla. Place on platter, cover with heated tomatillo sauce and top with sour cream and guacamole (mashed seasoned avocado). Serves 1.

Tomatillo Sauce

4   pounds tomatillos
2   pounds bell pepper
1   pound onions
3   jalapeños
1 ¼ cups water
¼   cup sugar
2   teaspoons salt
¼   teaspoon white pepper
½   teaspoon oregano

Grind tomatillos, bell peppers, onions and jalapeños together. Add remaining ingredients, mix well and bring to a boil. Simmer for about an hour. Makes about 1 gallon.

ENCHILADAS, SWEET SHOP

The *Sweet Shop* in Raton prepares enchiladas in a typical Southwest way.

2-3 corn tortillas per serving
Red chile sauce
Salad oil
Grated longhorn cheese
Diced onions
Chopped lettuce
Sliced tomatoes

58

Heat tortillas one at a time in about ½ inch hot oil. Place on heated plate. Top with red chile, then sprinkle with cheese and onions. Repeat with 2 more tortillas. Top with cheese. Heat under broiler to melt cheese. Decorate with lettuce and tomatoes.

Sauce

¼	cup pure ground red chile, medium hot
2	tablespoons flour
2	pounds lean ground meat
4	cups water
1½	teaspoons salt
1	teaspoon garlic powder
1	#300 can pinto beans
1	#300 can chile beans

Mix chile powder and flour together and lightly brown in oven at 300 degrees F for 10 minutes. Brown meat in large heavy saucepan and pour off excess fat. Stir flour/chile mixture into meat. Add water and cook gently until thick. Add beans and seasonings and simmer for about 20 minutes. Yields approximately ½ gallon of chile, which can be frozen for future use.

CLASSIC NEW MEXICO RED ENCHILADAS

12 blue corn tortillas
⅓ cup vegetable oil
3-4 cups red chile sauce (see page 7)
3 cups grated longhorn cheese
2 small onions, minced
4 eggs (optional)

Fry tortillas in oil until soft and drain on paper towels. Heat chile sauce. Layer tortillas on serving plates, topping each with grated cheese and minced onions and sauce. Stack 3 per serving plate and top with cheese and sauce. Put plates in oven to allow cheese to melt. Meanwhile, fry eggs in remaining oil. Top each enchilada stack with a fried egg. Serve immediately. Serves 4.

GREEN CHILE ENCHILADAS

6 blue corn tortillas
2 tablespoons oil
1 clove garlic
2 cups green chile sauce
1 tablespoon flour
2 cups grated longhorn or jack cheese
¼ cup minced onion
Salt to taste

Heat the tortillas on a hot griddle and keep warm under a tea towel. Heat the garlic in the oil, then discard garlic. Blend flour into oil. Stir in green chile sauce (see page 7 for recipe) and heat thoroughly. If mixture is too thick, add water. Add salt to taste. Layer tortillas with sauce, minced onion and cheese on ovenproof plates. Sprinkle cheese on top. Place in oven to allow cheese to melt. Serves 2. For a real New Mexico touch, place a poached or fried egg on top. The egg has the quality of melding all the flavors.

TAME NEW MEXICO
GREEN ENCHILADAS

6 blue corn tortillas
⅓ cup vegetable oil
1 clove garlic
1 tablespoon flour
1 14-ounce can stewed tomatoes
1 4-ounce can chopped green chile
   or ½ cup frozen chopped green chile
½ pound grated jack or longhorn cheese
1 small onion, minced
2 eggs (optional)

60 Fry tortillas in oil until soft and drain on paper towels. Mince garlic and heat in heavy saucepan in 1 tablespoon of the oil. Blend in flour, add tomatoes and green chile, and simmer gently for about 5 minutes. Place a tortilla on ovenproof serving plate. Top with some onion and cheese and a dipper of sauce. Layer 3 tortillas this way on each plate, ending with cheese. Spoon remaining sauce on top. Put plates in 325-degree F oven to allow cheese to melt. Top each stack with an egg fried in the remaining oil. Serve immediately. Serves 2.

GREEN CHILE STEW

Rosella Frederick of Cochiti is known for her good cooking. One of her specialties is her green chile stew. For feast days, she usually makes enormous pots of stew outside over an open fire in order not to heat up her spotless kitchen. She has cut down her recipe to family size for us.

2   pounds lean chuck
Lard or cooking oil
½   medium onion, chopped
4   medium potatoes (optional)
4   medium zucchini (optional)
12 large green chiles, roasted, peeled
     and cut in pieces **or** 1 7-ounce container
     frozen chopped green chile **or** 2 4-ounce
     cans chopped green chile
1   teaspoon garlic salt
1   teaspoon salt
6-7 cups water

Cut the meat up into very small pieces — about ½-inch cubes — and brown in a little oil in a large, deep heavy pan. Add the onions. Peel and dice the potatoes and brown them with the meat. (Rosella does not flour the meat because it makes the stew too thick for her family's taste.) When the meat and onion and potatoes (if used) have been browned, drain off any excess fat. Add the zucchini, if used, the chiles, garlic salt, salt and water. Bring to a boil and simmer for at least a half hour. Ladle into bowls and serve with homemade bread. The stew should be eaten with a spoon, like a hearty soup. Serves 6.

PUEBLO RED CHILE STEW

This recipe comes from Santa Clara Pueblo from the Joseph Lonewolf family.

10 pounds stew beef
2 gallons water
2 tablespoons salt
5 pounds potatoes
2 cups red chile powder
½ cup blue cornmeal

62 Cut meat in 1-inch cubes. Cover with water and bring to a boil in a large kettle. Reduce heat to simmer and cook, covered, for about 4 hours. Meanwhile, peel and cube potatoes. Add potatoes and salt and cook for 1½ hours. Measure red chile powder and cornmeal into bowl with enough cold water to make a paste. Stir slowly into stew. Mix in well, to thicken broth. Simmer for a half hour, then keep warm. Theresa Lonewolf figures on serving about 75 people on a feast day, but of course not everyone eats a lot of any one dish. If this were the main dish at a picnic or supper, it might serve 25 to 35 persons.

PUEBLO GREEN CHILE STEW

The Lonewolfs use the same recipe to make their green chile stew as they do their red. They eliminate the potatoes, however.

10 pounds stew beef
2   gallons water
2   tablespoons salt
5   cups chopped peeled green chile
2   teaspoons garlic powder
½   cup blue cornmeal

Cook meat as for red chile stew. Then add the green chile, salt and garlic powder. Mix the cornmeal in a little cold water and stir in rapidly. When mixture has thickened, simmer for about 45 minutes to let the flavors blend. Some families like to add cooked pinto beans during the last part of the cooking. Serve in soup bowls.

63

CHILES RELLENOS

Albuquerque's *El Pinto* is noted for its tasty native dishes, of which this is just one.

8 green chiles, roasted and peeled
1 cup jack cheese, cubed
2 eggs, beaten
½ cup flour
½ teaspoon salt
Cooking oil

Select full-bodied, firm straight chiles, allowing 2 per person. Wash and dry. Cut the tip end from each pod to prevent its bursting and roast and peel according to directions on page 6. After seeds and veins have been removed, fill each chile with cheese. Roll in mixture of flour and salt. Dip in beaten eggs. Fry in moderately hot oil until golden brown. Serve with refried beans and Spanish rice. Serves 4.

MENUDO

6 pounds tripe, well washed
2 onions, chopped
3 quarts water
1 clove garlic
1 teaspoon oregano
1 tablespoon salt

Put tripe in large heavy pan, add water and seasonings and bring to a boil. Simmer for 6 to 8 hours. When tripe is tender, cut in strips and return to pot.

In New Mexico, they say menudo is the breakfast of champions. But those who love it will eat it for any meal of the day.

65

RED CHILE BURRITOS

From Angie M. Garcia comes another of her specialties — the beloved burrito.

4   cups cooked pinto beans
2   teaspoons bacon fat or vegetable shortening
Garlic salt to taste
12 flour tortillas ⅛ to ¼ inch thick
1   cup grated jack or longhorn cheese
½ cup minced onion
Red chile sauce (see page 7)

Mash beans and season with garlic salt to taste. Fry in bacon fat. Heat tortillas on ungreased griddle and cover with towel to keep warm. Spoon hot bean mixture down the center of each tortilla, roll, and place 2 on each serving plate. Pour heated red chile sauce over burritos and top with cheese and onions. Serves 6.

CHALUPAS

Vegetable oil
6   *large corn tortillas*
1   *cup refried beans*
Salsa to taste
½   *cup minced onion*
1   *cup grated longhorn cheese*
1 ½ *cups shredded lettuce*
1   *medium tomato, chopped*
1 ½ *cups guacamole*
½   *cup sour cream*
Ripe olives

66

Fry tortillas one at a time in hot oil. Hold down in fat with wooden spoon so tortilla becomes saucer shaped. Drain on paper towels. Mix bottled or homemade salsa with beans to taste. Spread each tortilla with bean mixture, sprinkle with onions and cover with grated cheese. Place in 375-degree F oven for about 10 minutes. Use a cookie sheet or ovenproof plates. To serve, top each tortilla with lettuce and tomatoes. Spoon guacamole (mashed seasoned ripe avocado) on top. Decorate with a spoonful of sour cream and ripe olive slices. Serve immediately. Serves 6.

CHALUPAS EL PARAGUA

In Española's *El Paragua*, Luis and Frances Atencio make chalupas this way.

1 corn tortilla
Vegetable oil
¼ cup refried beans
Shredded chicken
¼ cup grated longhorn cheese
¼ cup guacamole
Shredded lettuce
¼ tomato
2 tablespoons sour cream
Black olives
Onion rings
Paprika

Fry the tortilla and place on an ovenproof plate. Spread with refried beans, then chicken, then cheese. Slide under broiler to melt cheese. Quickly cover with guacamole (mashed seasoned ripe avocado), lettuce, tomato cut in bits, and sour cream. Decorate with black olives and Bermuda or Spanish onion rings. Dust cream with paprika. Serve immediately. Serves 1.

CARNE ADOVADA

This recipe for pork marinated in chile sauce is an old New Mexico favorite. Angie M. Garcia recommends this method of making it.

24 *dry chile pods*
1   *tablespoon salt*
4   *cloves garlic*
1   *tablespoon oregano leaves*
3½ *cups water*
10 *lean pork chops or steaks*

Remove stems and seeds from chile pods. Place on cookie sheet and roast in oven at 250 degrees F for 3 to 4 minutes, turning frequently to prevent their burning. Rinse and drain pods. Blend a few at a time with water, garlic, salt and oregano in electric blender. When sauce is smooth, pour over pork in a large bowl and marinate for 24 hours. To cook, spread pork and sauce in a baking dish or roasting pan and bake at 350 degrees F for 1½ hours. Serves 10 (or 5 if the steaks are small).

TAMALES

There's no getting around it — making tamales takes a lot of work. But for those who love them, there's nothing to compare with a fresh homemade tamál.

5 pounds pork shoulder
1 clove garlic
¼ to ½ cup ground red chile
½ teaspoon ground oregano
1 tablespoon flour
Water
6 cups masa harina
½ cup lard
2 teaspoons salt
1 pound dried corn husks

69

Cover the pork with water, add the garlic, and bring to a boil. Simmer gently, covered, until meat is tender. Cool slightly. Discard the garlic. Chop the meat and set aside. Mix the chile powder, oregano and flour with 2 cups of the meat stock and add this to the chopped meat. Bring to a boil and simmer gently until mixture is thick. Cool. Beat the lard until it is light and fluffy. Blend in the masa. Then add enough meat stock or water to make the mixture soft and pliable. You should be able to spread it easily, but it shouldn't be soupy. Soak the husks in hot water until they are soft. Drain. Spread a thin layer of masa on a husk. Put a heaping tablespoon of the meat mixture down the center of the masa. Roll the husk carefully around the meat filling. Wrap another husk from the opposite side. Don't squish them! Tie the ends with string. Stand the tamales on their ends on a layer of corn husks in a steamer or blancher. Steam for about an hour. Drain and serve with more red chile sauce and beans.

FEAST DAY POSOLE

When the Joseph Lonewolf family of Santa Clara Pueblo prepares for feast day, this is the way they make their posole.

10 pounds beef, cooked tender
1 gallon can hominy
1 gallon water
1 large bunch carrots, sliced thinly
2 cups celery, diced with tops
1 cup diced bell pepper
1 cup green onions, diced with tops
1 tablespoon garlic powder
1 tablespoon onion salt
1 tablespoon dried wild celery
  or 1 teaspoon celery salt

Rinse hominy in cold water, then put into 3-gallon kettle with 1 gallon water. Long cooking at a low simmer ensures tender corn. When it is soft but not falling apart, add meat, which has been cooked tender. (Sometimes Theresa Lonewolf uses a pressure cooker for the meat.) Add remaining ingredients and simmer gently for 15 minutes. Correct seasoning. Wild celery can be picked in the spring and dried. It adds a special and delectable flavor. This recipe may be halved. It freezes well.

POSOLE ORTIZ

Everyone has his own special recipe for posole. This is the way Willie and June Ortiz prepare it at *La Tertulia* in Santa Fe — and good it is.

2 cups frozen white posole (hominy)
1 quart water
1 pound pork shoulder or chops
⅛ teaspoon oregano
1 teaspoon whole black peppercorns
⅓ cup chopped onion
4 dried red chile peppers, crumbled
Salt

Mix all ingredients in a large, heavy pot. Bring to a boil and simmer, covered, for about 2½ hours or until the kernels are soft but not mushy. Salt to taste. Serves 4.

THE SHED'S POSOLE STEW

1 pound lean pork shoulder
2 pounds frozen posole (hominy)
Juice of one lime
2 tablespoons coarse red chile
3 cloves garlic
¼ teaspoon dried oregano
3 tablespoons salt

Cook the pork in a pressure cooker, with water to cover, for 20 minutes. Reduce pressure under cold water. Open pot and add posole, lime juice and chile. Add water — about twice as much as the amount of posole. Cook for 45 minutes under pressure. →

Reduce pressure under cold water. Remove the pork and cut up. Put posole, pork, garlic, oregano and salt in a large, heavy covered pot and simmer for 1 to 3 hours, or until hominy kernels have burst and are soft but not mushy. Serve alone or as a side dish. Freezes well. Note: These times are set for Santa Fe's high altitude. At lower altitudes, where the boiling point is higher, you may wish to try shorter cooking times at first.

CHICOS

Chicos are sweet corn kernels that have been dried and saved for winter. This dish is popular in the Spanish-speaking villages of northern New Mexico.

2 cups chicos
10 cups water
2 pounds pork
1 onion, minced
1 clove garlic
½ teaspoon oregano
4 chile pods
2 teaspoons salt

Wash chicos and soak overnight. Drain and cover with 5 cups of water. Bring to a boil and simmer for about an hour. Meanwhile, cut pork in 1-inch cubes and fry until brown. Drain fat. Stir in a cup or 2 of water (to gather up the flavorful bits at the bottom of the pan). Pour meat, garlic, oregano, washed and crushed chile pods, salt to taste and remaining water in with chicos. Cover and simmer for 2½ hours or until chicos are tender. (Or use the pressure cooker and cook for about 1 hour.) Serve in soup bowls. Serves 6.

PHILOMENA'S FLAUTAS

Where once the security guard's station stood at the entrance to Los Alamos is now a well-known New Mexico restaurant — *Philomena's.* Flautas are crisp rolled corn tortillas filled with meat.

Vegetable oil
Corn tortillas — 3 per serving
Leftover cooked beef, chicken or turkey
Guacamole
Sour cream
Parmesan cheese
Shredded lettuce
Chopped tomatoes
Ripe olives
Salsa

Soften tortillas in hot vegetable oil. Drain on paper towels. Along the center of each tortilla put a spoonful or two of minced cooked meat. Bring the edges of the tortilla to the center and overlap. Place finished side down in hot oil and fry until crisp. Drain and place 3 on each serving plate. Spread with guacamole (mashed seasoned ripe avocado) and sour cream. Sprinkle with cheese and garnish with lettuce, tomatoes and ripe olives. Serve with hot sauce (salsa). Good with Spanish rice and refried beans.

TACOS, SHED STYLE

To many a visitor to New Mexico, *The Shed* in Santa Fe epitomizes all the mouth-watering attributes of New Mexico cooking at its finest. And there are those who say if you haven't had lunch at *The Shed*, you haven't been to Santa Fe.

1   pound lean ground beef
12 blue corn tortillas
1   cup homemade chile sauce
    or canned enchilada sauce
1   pound longhorn cheese, grated
Chopped lettuce
Chopped onions
Chopped tomatoes
Cooking oil

74

Brown the ground beef in a heavy skillet and drain off all grease. Mix in the chile sauce. Fry tortillas quickly in hot oil until they are limp. Drain. Allowing 2 to a plate (use oven-safe plates), place 2 tablespoons of the meat mixture on each tortilla. Add spoonfuls of the cheese, lettuce, onions and tomatoes. Fold tortilla over and sprinkle with more grated cheese. Place in 425-degree F oven until the cheese melts. Serves 6.

DELLA'S TACOS

Della's Spanish Dining Room in Farmington is one of the most popular restaurants in northwestern New Mexico. But Della Chavez throws up her hands in dismay and laughs at the idea of writing down her recipes. One must watch to see how it is done, she says. This is how she prepares her tacos.

Take ground chuck and brown it in the frying pan, draining off excess fat. One pound of meat will probably fill six tortillas. Season the meat with *salsa* — made with chopped peeled tomatoes, garlic, salt, chopped onions, chopped red chiles. (The quantities, Della implies, will depend on one's own taste.)

When the meat is ready, warm tortillas on a grill. Place in a bowl and cover with a towel. They'll steam themselves soft. Fold the tortillas in half and stuff with meat. Pin with wooden toothpicks.

Fry the tacos in very hot deep fat (perhaps 375-400 degrees F) for just a minute. Turn over, then remove and drain. Remove toothpicks and stuff with grated longhorn cheese (perhaps a half pound for 6 tacos), shredded lettuce and finely chopped tomatoes, in that order. Serve.

CHILE CON CARNE

Angie M. Garcia makes her chile stew with pork and suggests this method.

4 pounds pork shoulder
18 dry red chile pods
2 cloves garlic
1 teaspoon salt
3 cups water

Remove stems and seeds from chile pods. Place pods in oven at 250 degrees F for about 3 minutes. Turn frequently so they don't burn. Rinse the pods in warm water and drain. Put the garlic cloves, salt and water in an electric blender with a few of the chile pods. Blend in the pods a few at a time until you have run them all and the mixture is smooth. Cut the pork roast into 1-inch cubes and fry them in a large heavy skillet. Drain off excess fat. Add chile sauce to cooked pork. Simmer, covered, for about 15 minutes. Makes about 2 quarts. Angie says the flavor of the chile is improved if you make it the day before you plan to serve it and then heat it up.

CHICKEN SOUR CREAM ENCHILADAS

12 corn tortillas
4   cups green chile sauce
3   cups minced cooked chicken
1   pound jack cheese, grated
¼   cup minced onion (optional)
Salt to taste
1   pint sour cream

Heat tortillas on a hot griddle and keep warm under a tea towel. Or heat the tortillas in oil and drain well on paper towels. Mix one cup of the chile sauce (see page 7 for recipe) with the chicken. Put ¼ cup of the chicken mixture on each tortilla and roll it up. Place in an oblong baking dish. Cover the enchiladas with the grated cheese. Add the onion, if desired, and salt to taste to the remaining chile sauce and pour over the enchiladas. Bake at 350 degrees F for about 20 minutes. Smother with sour cream and return to oven for 10 minutes, or until everything is hot. Serve immediately. Serves 6.

NAVAJO BLOOD SAUSAGE

Like the Irish, Scots, Scandinavians, Poles, Bohemians and others, the Navajos make blood sausage. Each group uses the materials at hand, whether oatmeal, wheat, rice or barley. In the Southwest, it's cornmeal.

1 sheep's stomach
1 quart fresh sheep blood
½ cup stone-ground cornmeal
1 onion, minced
½ cup chopped green chile
    or hot yellow chile
½ cup stomach fat, chopped fine
Salt and pepper to taste

78

Scrub the stomach well in cold water and turn inside out. Mix blood, cornmeal, onion, chile and fat, and add salt and pepper to taste. Put mixture in the stomach and tie off into baseball-size sausages. Leave some air space in each sausage to allow room for expansion. Cover sausage with water in large kettle and simmer for about 4 hours. Larry King, who shared this recipe with us, recommends that the boiling be done outside because the smell can become overpowering in a small kitchen.

NAVAJO MUTTON STEW

Larry King shares with us his mother's recipe for making mutton stew.

2 pounds lean mutton or lamb
6 potatoes
1 bunch carrots
1 cup celery, sliced
1 onion, chopped (optional)
Salt and pepper to taste

Cut meat into cubes, trimming excess fat but leaving bones for flavor. Peel and cut up potatoes and carrots. Cover meat with water, add vegetables and bring to a boil. Simmer for 1 hour (or more, depending on whether it's lamb or mutton) until meat is tender. Add salt and pepper to taste. Serves 6.

If wild celery or wild carrots are available, use those. If a thicker stew is desired, grate half a potato into the pot. Because Navajo sheepherders are often many miles from stores, they don't have access to fresh vegetables and spices. This stew may therefore seem bland to our taste.

BLUE CORNMEAL RABBIT STEW

Rosella Frederick of Cochiti learned this very old recipe from
her grandmother. Originally, it was made with robins, Rosella
says, and sometimes it is made with doves. Wild rabbits have
more flavor than domesticated ones, Rosella says, but she uses
whatever is available.

1 rabbit, cut up
½ cup blue cornmeal
½ teaspoon salt

Cover the rabbit with water and bring to a boil. Simmer,
covered, until it is tender — about 45 minutes. Remove meat
and cool slightly. Set stock aside. Remove rabbit meat from
bones and return the meat to the stock. Mix the cornmeal and
salt into 2 cups of warm water, then stir rapidly into the rabbit
stock. Mix well, cover and simmer for another ½ hour. Serves
4 to 6.

VEAL OSCAR

The *Holiday Inn de Las Cruces* is probably the most unusual and beautiful Holiday Inn in the United States. Its restaurants attract local diners, as well as travelers, with recipes like this one.

4 ounces thinly sliced veal
¼ cup chablis
⅛ teaspoon ginger
⅛ teaspoon white pepper
¼ teaspoon salt
Flour
Olive oil
2 large asparagus spears, cooked
2 ounces crabmeat
2 tablespoons hollandaise sauce

Marinate sliced veal in chablis for about 20 minutes. Season wine with ginger, white pepper and salt. Roll veal in flour. Saute in olive oil for about 5 minutes. Remove and place on warm ovenproof plate. Place asparagus spears on top of veal. Heat crabmeat in butter and place over asparagus. Cover with hollandaise sauce. Reheat briefly in oven if necessary. Serves 1.

PAELLA WILD ROSE

Cosmopolitan cooking is not limited to the big cities in New Mexico. This recipe came from the *Wild Rose* in the small town of Pecos.

3 cut-up chickens
½ cup butter
2 pounds sausage meat (spicy)
2 onions
2 small yellow chiles
1 cooked carrot
2 celery stalks
2 cloves garlic
2 tablespoons olive oil
2 cans Italian plum tomatoes
6 ounces tomato paste
2 bay leaves
2 cups rice
4-5 cups chicken stock
Saffron (optional)
2 pounds shrimp
1 package "crab boil" seasoning
2 pounds clams

Brown chicken in butter. Brown sausage meat and drain well. Slice onions, chop chiles, puree carrot and celery stalks, mash garlic. Saute the vegetables in olive oil. Mix in Italian tomatoes, tomato paste and bay leaves. Simmer gently for about 15 minutes. Arrange chicken and sausage in ovenproof casserole, cover with sauce and bake at 325 degrees F for about one hour. Meanwhile cook the rice in chicken stock with a few threads of saffron, if available. Drop shrimp in boiling water with "crab boil" seasoning. Cook for only a minute, then drain. Steam the clams until they open. Do not overcook. To serve: Arrange chicken and sausage on rice. Ring each serving with shrimp and top with a few clams in their shells. Decorate with a wedge of lemon and parsley. Serves 6 to 8.

CHUCKWAGON CHICKEN IN WINE

Another outdoors recipe that could be made at home in the kitchen as well.

2 whole chickens
Salt
Pepper
MSG
3 tablespoons butter
Olive oil
1 clove garlic
Mushrooms
1 cup dry white wine
1 onion, chopped

Disjoint chicken, dry thoroughly. Sprinkle with salt, pepper and MSG. Over *low* fire, melt some butter and about 2 table-spoons olive oil in a large skillet. When quite hot, throw in one clove garlic and saute chicken until golden brown, about 10 minutes each side. Knock down the fire and cover skillet. In separate pan, saute onion in olive oil with two handfuls mush-rooms until mushrooms are soft. Spread mixture over chicken, add dry wine, cover tightly. Simmer 30-40 minutes. Serves 4-6.

POJARSKI

The Periscope in Santa Fe is known throughout the Southwest for its menu, which changes daily, and for its cosmopolitan cooking. Here is a sample, a delicate chicken dish.

1 ¾ *pounds chicken breasts*
10 *thin slices white bread, crusts removed*
½ *cup heavy cream*
¾ *cup unsalted butter*
1 *teaspoon salt*
¼ *teaspoon ground white pepper*
1 *egg*
1 *teaspoon water*
1 *teaspoon vegetable oil*
Fine breadcrumbs
Butter
Hollandaise sauce

Cut the meat into very small pieces and chop it by hand or in a blender or Cuisinart until it is a fine paste. Shred the bread and soak it in the cream. With the mixer still on creaming speed, add the meat, 2 or 3 tablespoons at a time. Add the soaked bread, bit by bit, and last, the salt and pepper. Continue beating until the mixture is homogenous.

By hand, shape 18 cutlets about ½ inch thick. Flour the cutlets, brush with anglaise (one egg beaten with one teaspoon water and one teaspoon oil), and coat with fine breadcrumbs. Saute the cutlets in clarified butter until golden on both sides. Serve with hollandaise sauce. Makes 9 servings.

TERIYAKI MARINADE, LOS ARCOS

Los Arcos, in Truth or Consequences, marinates chicken in this marvelous teriyaki sauce. But you could also use it for steak or fish.

1 *bunch (about 6 or 8) green onions*
3 *ounces fresh ginger root*
2 *cloves garlic*
2 *cups soy sauce*
⅓ *cup dry sherry*
½ *cup soybean oil*
½ *cup brown sugar*
½ *cup white sugar*

Grind onions with peeled ginger root and garlic cloves. Mix with other ingredients in a large, heavy saucepan. Stir ingredients over heat until dissolved then bring to a boil and allow to cool overnight in refrigerator. Strain off excess vegetables. Marinate chicken in sauce for 2 hours or longer. (Overnight in the refrigerator is fine.) Baste with butter and charbroil.

MOUSSAKA
(Greek Eggplant Casserole)

Albuquerque's annual Greek festival sponsored by the St. George Greek Orthodox Church has become a major event in the city. Dishes like this one are served to the eager and hungry guests.

3   medium eggplants, sliced lengthwise
½   cup olive or salad oil
1   pound ground beef
1   teaspoon cinnamon
¼   teaspoon ground cloves
½   teaspoon ground allspice
1   teaspoon sugar
1   9-ounce can tomato sauce
Salt and pepper to taste
1 ½ cups grated Romano cheese

Soak sliced eggplant in salt water about 10 minutes to remove bitterness. Pat dry and fry eggplants in hot oil until brown. Drain and set aside. Brown beef in frying pan until well browned, then add spices and tomato sauce. Simmer gently for about 10 minutes. Cover bottom of a roasting pan with half the browned eggplants. Add all of beef, sprinkle half the grated cheese over ground beef. Add remaining eggplants on top. Top with sauce:

Sauce

3   eggs, well beaten
½ cup water
2   tablespoons flour

Blend well and pour slowly over eggplant casserole. Add remaining cheese and bake uncovered in 350-degree F oven for about 30 minutes or until browned.

ZUCCHINI MONTOYA

Patricia Montoya recommends this meal-in-a-dish casserole.

6   medium zucchini
½   pound ground beef
½   pound pork sausage
3½ cups soft white bread (torn in small pieces)
1¾ cups longhorn cheese, grated
1   small onion, minced
2   eggs, beaten
2   tablespoons butter
1   teaspoon salt

Wash, dice and simmer zucchini in about ½ cup water in a tightly covered pan until soft. In a large skillet, fry ground beef and sausage until done. Drain excess fat. Mix squash (including water used in cooking) with meat. Let mixture cool for about 5 minutes. Add all remaining ingredients except for about ¼ cup of the cheese. Mix well. Turn into a 1½-quart casserole, sprinkle with remaining cheese and bake at 350 degrees F for 30 minutes. Serves 4.

CHUCKWAGON LASAGNA

Although this recipe is geared for outdoor cooking, it can as easily be baked in the oven in your kitchen.

1 ½ pounds ground beef
½   cup chopped onion
1   clove garlic
½   pound lasagna noodles
1   can (6 ounces) tomato paste
1   can (6 ounces) tomato sauce
1   can (1 pound) tomatoes
1   teaspoon salt
¼   teaspoon pepper
¼   teaspoon basil
½   teaspoon oregano
½   pound Mozarella cheese
½   cup Parmesan cheese
1   large carton cottage cheese

Brown beef, onion and garlic. Boil lasagna noodles. Add to beef: tomato paste, tomato sauce, tomatoes, salt, pepper, basil and oregano. Cook 15 minutes. Grease dutch oven. Layer in oven as follows: tomato-beef mixture, Parmesan cheese, noodles, Mozarella cheese, cottage cheese. Repeat layers until ingredients are used up. Cover and bake for about one hour. After 30 minutes be sure to place new coals on and under the dutch oven. Serves 6.

CLOVIS STEAK SANDWICH

1 small flank steak
2 long French rolls
   or large onion rolls
Butter
1 cup frijoles refritos (mashed refried beans)
½ cup grated longhorn cheese
1 avocado
¼ teaspoon garlic salt
1 teaspoon minced onion
1 tomato, diced
Taco sauce (optional)
Onion salt
Pepper

89

Broil the flank steak to the desired degree of doneness. Split, butter and heat the rolls. Slice the steak in thin slices on the diagonal and arrange on the bottom halves of the rolls. Cover with beans and sprinkle with cheese. Return to oven to let the cheese melt. Meanwhile, mash the avocado with garlic salt and mix in minced onion and tomato. Spread this on top of the bean mixture, season with taco sauce, onion salt and pepper, cover with top half of roll and dig in. Serves 2.

WESTERN BEEF STEW

The *Eklund Hotel* in Clayton is known for its authentic Victorian decor as well as its taste-tempting meals. The secret of success in this recipe is in cooking each vegetable to its desired tenderness while retaining the proper firmness.

1 pound cooked beef chunks
1 tablespoon Worcestershire sauce
1 11-ounce can tomatoes
8 carrots
1 large onion
4 medium potatoes
½ cup chopped celery
2½ cups water or beef bouillon
1 tablespoon flour
1 teaspoon gravy base

Brown beef chunks in Worcestershire. Set aside. Cook each of the cut-up vegetables separately until tender but not mushy. For gravy use a commercial soup base but a substitute may be made by stirring flour and gravy base into 1 cup of cold water until lumps disappear. Heat remaining water or bouillon. Stir in thickening. Simmer gently for five minutes. Add cooked vegetables, meat and tomatoes. Add salt and pepper to taste. Heat thoroughly but do not cook. Serves 4.

OVEN BARBECUED BRISKET

This was a specialty on a famous ranch near Lincoln.

1 4-5 pound brisket of beef
¾ cup tomato puree
1 teaspoon Worcestershire sauce
1 teaspoon vinegar
½ teaspoon sugar
2 tablespoons vegetable oil
½ teaspoon thyme
½ teaspoon dry mustard
¼ teaspoon liquid smoke
Salt or garlic salt and pepper to taste

Place meat on a large sheet of heavy foil and place on baking sheet. Combine remaining ingredients in a saucepan and bring to a boil. Pour sauce over meat. Bring up the foil and fold it so that the meat is sealed in. Bake at 350 degrees F for 2-3 hours, or until meat is tender. Serves 6.

MATAMBRE

Another choice recipe from the *Wild Rose* in Pecos.

2 2-pound flank steaks
2 cups red wine
Herbs
6 carrots
6 eggs
1 pound fresh spinach
1 Bermuda onion
Salt and pepper
Chile pequins

→

Marinate the flank steaks in wine and herbs of your choice for at least 2 hours. Butterfly the steaks, place them end to end on a sheet of foil, and pound the edges together so that you have one long thin piece of meat. Meanwhile, steam the carrots, hardboil the eggs, slice the onion thinly and wash the spinach well. Lay the vegetables and eggs on the steak. Cover with marinade and sprinkle with chile pequins, salt and pepper. Roll as tightly as possible and secure with strings. Wrap in the foil and place in a pan with about an inch of water. Roast at 350 degrees F for 1 hour. Remove foil and string and slice to serve. Serves 8.

92 MUSHROOM SAUCE FOR STEAK

The Double Eagle in Old Mesilla, near Las Cruces, like the other restaurants in the Tinnie chain, is known for its sumptuous surroundings and good food, simply prepared. This mushroom sauce adds the final fillip to a fine steak.

6 large mushrooms, sliced
1 tablespoon butter
¼ cup dry sherry
Steak seasoning

Saute the mushrooms in butter. Pour in sherry. Mix in a liberal dash of your favorite bottled steak seasoning. Reheat and pour over steak just before serving. Serves 1.

FETTINE DI MANZO ALLA PIZZAIOLA

The *Casa Vieja* in Corrales shared this recipe for an Italian specialty with us.

6 ripe tomatoes
4 cloves garlic
2 tablespoons dried oregano
1 cup dry white wine
Salt and pepper

4 one-inch-thick sirloin steaks
¼ cup olive oil
1 cup grated Romano cheese

93

Peel tomatoes by dropping them in simmering water for a couple of minutes. When the skins begin to split, remove tomatoes and peel with a sharp knife. Mash tomatoes. Chop garlic finely. Mix tomatoes, garlic, oregano and white wine in a heavy saucepan. Bring to a boil and simmer for about 15 minutes. Add salt and pepper to taste.

Trim all the fat from steaks. Lightly flatten to about ¾ of an inch between sheets of waxed paper with a cutlet bat or the side of a heavy cleaver. Saute the steaks in hot olive oil for about 3 minutes on each side. Remove to an oven-proof platter. Cover with the sauce and generously sprinkle with freshly grated Romano cheese. Broil in a preheated broiler until nicely browned — about 3 minutes. Serve immediately with spaghetti dressed with olive oil and garlic. A stout red wine goes very nicely with this. Serves 4.

DOLMADES
(Stuffed Grape Leaves)

1 jar grape leaves
1 tablespoon butter or olive oil
1 medium onion, minced
1 pound ground beef or lamb
½ cup rice
1 tablespoon parsley, minced
1 egg, beaten
1 teaspoon oregano
1 tablespoon mint, minced
Salt and pepper to taste
2 tablespoons butter

94

Saute onion in butter until soft. Mix in meat, rice, parsley, egg, oregano, mint, salt and pepper. Cook for about 10 minutes. Take 1 teaspoon of filling and place in center of 1 large leaf or 2 small ones, being sure that the shiny side of the leaf is underneath, or on outside when rolled. Carefully fold over top and sides like an envelope and roll up like a miniature football. Place a few coarse leaves in bottom of pot. Carefully arrange the balls on top, side by side, and in layers until all filling and leaves are used. Add 2 cups water and butter. Place heavy plate on top and simmer for a half hour or longer if needed.

Egg Lemon Sauce

4 eggs
¼ cup lemon juice
Broth from dolmades pot

Beat eggs until light and fluffy, add lemon juice slowly, beating constantly. Add hot broth gradually, continuing the beating. Pour slowly over grape leaves in pot, shaking pot gently so that sauce covers all grape leaf rolls. Allow to settle several minutes before serving. Serves 4 to 6.

SILK-WEAVERS LAMB

David Henkel of La Puebla in northern New Mexico is always the hit of the evening when he brings this succulent lamb dish to potluck parties.

4 pounds lamb (from leg)
1 cup yogurt
½ cup grated onions
½ teaspoon ground cloves (optional)
4 cups water
4 chicken bouillon cubes
8 garlic cloves
¾ teaspoon ground ginger
½ teaspoon ground black pepper
1 teaspoon ground cinnamon
1 teaspoon ground coriander
¼ cup fresh ground coconut
    or unsweetened moist-pack coconut
3 tablespoons vegetable oil
1 medium onion, thinly sliced
2 teaspoons fennel seed
1 tablespoon chopped parsley
Juice of 1 lime

Slice or cube lamb and place in large mixing bowl with yogurt and grated onion. Mix well and set aside for at least 1 hour. (Or, covered, in refrigerator overnight.) Optional: add ½ teaspoon ground cloves. Place water, bouillon, garlic, ginger, pepper, cinnamon, coriander and coconut in a large heavy pan. Bring to a boil then simmer for 5 minutes. Meanwhile, heat vegetable oil in a large heavy skillet or dutch oven. Add sliced onion and fennel seed, and fry until crisp. Add the lamb-yogurt mixture and continue frying until the meat separates from the yogurt — about 10 to 15 minutes. Add the bouillon mixture. Cover and let simmer until the gravy is reduced to half its original volume and the meat is tender (approximately 2 hours). Serve in a shallow dish. Sprinkle with lime juice and parsley. Serve with brown rice. Mango chutney, sliced toasted almonds and raisins should be available as condiments. Serves 8.

TIROPETA
(Greek Cheese Pie)

This is another recipe from Albuquerque's St. George Greek Orthodox Church.

6 eggs
1 pound Ricotta cheese
½ cup grated Mozarella cheese
½ cup grated sharp cheese
½ cup grated Parmesan cheese
½ teaspoon salt
1 cup (½ pound) sweet butter, melted
1 pound filo*

96

In a 9 x 13 pan, layer about 15 sheets of filo, buttering each. Beat eggs, cheeses and salt until well mixed. Use electric beater. If too thick, add a little milk. Pour mixture over filo in pan. Layer about 15 sheets filo, buttering each layer, over cheese mixture. If any butter remains, pour over top of filo layer. Cut into diamond or square shapes. Bake in 350-degree F oven about an hour. This freezes well. You can pop in oven, heat and serve.

*Filo is special thin Greek pastry, obtainable at many delicatessen and specialty shops for gourmets.

DESSERTS

CREME DE MENTHE PARFAIT

From the *Double Eagle* in Old Mesilla comes this recipe for a
dessert that is deceptively simple, devastatingly good.

2   *4-ounce scoops vanilla ice cream*
1 ½ *ounces crème de menthe*
1   *green maraschino or candied cherry*

Place ice cream in chilled parfait glass. Pour crème de menthe
over ice cream. Place cherry on top. Serves 1.

CHRISTINA'S ALWAYS-PERFECT FLAN

Here is a foolproof version of that favorite Spanish and New Mexican dessert, the baked caramelized custard.

½ cup sugar
8 egg yolks
2 egg whites
1 14-ounce can sweetened condensed milk
1 13-ounce can evaporated milk
2 cups whole milk or water
1 teaspoon vanilla

In a heavy skillet, melt sugar, stirring constantly. When it is light brown, pour it into a 2-quart mold. Tip mold quickly in all directions so that caramel coats the inside. (It will get very hot, so hold it with tongs.) Set mold aside. Beat eggs until thick. Beat in condensed milk, evaporated milk, milk (or water) and vanilla. Pour into the prepared mold. Cover securely with a tight lid or with 3 layers of foil tied down. Place on rack in pressure cooker with 2 to 3 cups of water (follow manufacturer's directions) and cook for 20 minutes after control jiggles. (Try 25 minutes at higher altitudes.) Cool rapidly. After custard is chilled, turn out on serving platter. Serves 12.

FLAN ATENCIO

This is the way Frances Atencio makes her flan at *El Paragua* in Española.

1 ¾ cups sugar
3   egg whites
8   egg yolks
2   large (13-ounce) cans evaporated milk
2   teaspoons vanilla
6   tablespoons brandy or rum (optional)

Put 1 cup of the sugar into a deep baking pan or loaf pan. Place over heat and, stirring constantly with a wooden spoon, melt sugar. When it turns golden brown, remove from heat and tilt pan so caramel coats the inside evenly. Cool. Meanwhile, beat egg whites and yolks with remaining sugar, milk and vanilla. Strain mixture into the caramel-coated pan. Cover with lid or foil. Place pan in a larger pan containing an inch of hot water. Bake at 350 degrees F for an hour. To serve, turn onto a serving platter. For a spectacular presentation, Frances pours warmed brandy or rum over the custard and lights it to send it to the table aflame. Serves 8 to 12.

TOCINA DEL CIELO

This is one of those sweet morsels so loved in Spain and Mexico. A very small portion tops off a perfect dinner. Serve along with tiny cups of black coffee.

½ cup sugar
6 egg yolks
2 egg whites
1 14-ounce can sweetened condensed milk
1 13-ounce can evaporated milk
1 teaspoon vanilla

Melt sugar in heavy pan, stirring constantly. When syrup is light brown, pour into 8-inch or 9-inch square pan. With wooden spoon, spread around evenly in bottom and on sides, tilting the pan as you work. (Use tongs or a hot potholder!) Set this pan aside in a larger pan with about an inch of water in it. Beat egg yolks and whites. Beat in condensed milk, evaporated milk and vanilla. Pour into prepared pan. Cover with foil and bake at 350 degrees F for about 45 minutes or until mixture has set. Cool. Turn out on platter and cut in small squares to serve. Makes about 20 small servings. Sometimes the dessert is cut in 1-inch cubes and served with toothpicks on a dessert tray.

NATILLAS

This is a very old dish, and is very similar to floating island. Mary Ortiz has given us this recipe.

4 *eggs, separated*
¼ cup flour
1 quart rich milk
¾ cup sugar
⅛ teaspoon salt
½ teaspoon vanilla

Make a paste of the egg yolks, flour and 1 cup of the milk. Add sugar and salt to the rest of the milk and scald. Stir milk gradually into egg mixture and return to saucepan. Cook slowly, stirring constantly, until the mixture has become thickened — about 30 minutes. (This could also be done in the top of a double boiler over hot water.) Remove from heat, stir in vanilla and let cool. Beat egg whites until they are stiff but not dry. Fold into custard. Chill before serving. Garnish with nutmeg if desired. Serves 6 to 8.

MOCHA DESSERT

The most popular restaurant dessert in New Mexico, this "secret" recipe originated in a famous Santa Fe restaurant and has spread throughout the Southwest. This is one version. Forget calories and carbohydrates when you taste it.

2 tablespoons butter
2 tablespoons cornstarch
1 cup strong coffee
3 1-ounce squares semisweet chocolate
5 eggs, separated
½ cup + 3 tablespoons sugar
1 teaspoon vanilla
⅛ teaspoon salt
1 cup chocolate wafer crumbs
Whipped cream

Work butter and cornstarch together in top of double boiler until you have a smooth paste. Add coffee. Cook over — not in — hot water, stirring constantly until the butter has melted. Add chocolate and continue cooking and stirring until mixture is smooth and thickened. Beat egg yolks until thick and light, gradually adding the ½ cup sugar as you beat. Pour a little of the chocolate mixture into the egg yolks and continue beating. Add all chocolate mixture and then return to top of double boiler. Cook and stir over boiling water for about 7 to 10 minutes, or until mixture is thick and smooth. Stir in vanilla and cool slightly. Meanwhile, beat egg whites and salt until thick and frothy. Add remaining 3 tablespoons of sugar gradually and beat until mixture holds a point. Fold egg whites into chocolate mixture until mixture is well blended. In a buttered 8-inch-square pan sprinkle about ⅓ of the chocolate wafer crumbs. (About a half package of chocolate wafers will grind down into 1 cup of fine crumbs.) Pour in half of the chocolate mixture evenly. Sprinkle with ⅓ of the crumbs and cover with remaining chocolate mixture. Sprinkle with remaining crumbs. Cover and freeze. To serve, cut in squares and top with whipped cream. Serves 9 to 12, depending on how large you make the portions.

PANOCHA

This classic recipe for a sprouted wheat flour pudding is not unlike the Indian pudding of New England. Panocha flour is also known as *harina enraizada* or sprouted wheat flour. It may be found in specialty shops, Cuban or Mexican groceries or health food stores. This recipe comes from Martha Montoya.

4 *cups panocha flour*
2 *cups sifted white flour*
½ *teaspoon salt*
2 *cones* piloncillo *(Mexican brown sugar)*
   or *1 cup brown sugar, packed*
6 *cups warm water*

104

In a large ovenproof bowl, mix panocha flour, sifted white flour and salt. Slowly stir in water until mixture is very soft. Add shaved *piloncillo* or brown sugar and mix until completely dissolved. Cover bowl with lid or foil and place in 350-degree F oven. Bake for 1½ hours. Panocha is done when it turns a dark brown and is thick in consistency. Serve hot or cold, with or without cream. Like Indian pudding, panocha is at its most delectable when it is served hot with ice cream melting on top. Serves 10 to 12.

HARVEST TORTE

From southern New Mexico, where pecans and apples thrive, comes this old-fashioned dessert.

4 cups diced unpeeled tart apples
1 cup sugar
½ cup sifted flour
2 teaspoons baking powder
1 egg, lightly beaten
1 tablespoon melted butter
1 teaspoon vanilla
½ cup coarsely chopped pecans

Preheat oven to 400 degrees F. Place the apples in a mixing bowl. Sift together the sugar, flour and baking powder and pour over the apples. Mix the egg, butter and vanilla and add with the pecans. Stir thoroughly. Pour the mixture into a greased 8-inch square pan and bake 40 minutes or until apples are tender. Serve hot or cold with cream or ice cream. Serves 6.

SOPA

Martha Montoya has shared her recipe with us for this classic bread pudding that is made in almost every Spanish and Pueblo kitchen in New Mexico. *Sopa* means soup — and "dry soups" are not uncommon in Latin countries where they are often, like this one, a dessert. This pudding is also called *capirotada* in New Mexico.

1   *large loaf white bread**
1 ½ *pounds longhorn cheese, thinly sliced*
1   *cup raisins*

2   *cups brown sugar, packed*
2 ½ *quarts water*
1   *tablespoon cinnamon*
1   *tablespoon butter*

Lightly toast the bread slices. Soak the raisins in warm water until they are puffy. In a large ovenproof baking dish, layer the slices of bread, the cheese and the raisins, starting with the bread and repeating the layers until the ingredients are used up. In a large saucepan, dissolve the brown sugar and cinnamon in water. Add butter. Bring to a boil and simmer for about 15 minutes. Pour the hot syrup slowly over the layers in the baking dish until all ingredients are completely soaked and covered. Cover dish with lid or foil. Bake in 350-degree F oven for 1 hour. Serve hot or cold, plain or with cream. Serves 8.

*Some people like to use up leftover dry cake instead of some of the bread. Pound cake is ideal.

SANTA CLARA BREAD PUDDING

In Santa Clara Pueblo, Theresa Lonewolf makes this adaptation of *sopa* for Feast Day.

2 *loaves long white sandwich bread*
2 *12-ounce packages sliced American cheese*
2 *10-ounce packages pecan halves*
1 *15-ounce box seedless raisins*
Cinnamon

5 *quarts water*
6 *cups sugar*
2 *tablespoons cinnamon*
½ *teaspoon nutmeg*
½ *cup vegetable shortening*

Toast bread slices. Into a large ungreased covered roasting pan put a layer of toasted bread torn into bite size pieces. Layer over that strips of cheese. Sprinkle with chopped pecans, raisins and cinnamon until roaster is heaped. Push down with hands and fill as full as possible. Cover roaster and make syrup by boiling water, sugar, cinnamon, nutmeg and shortening together for 30 minutes. Dip syrup from saucepan over pudding. This is a two-woman job. Usually Theresa dips and one of the girls stirs the boiling syrup into the pudding. When syrup has been stirred well into pudding, put roaster lid on at once. The steam will cook the pudding perfectly. It isn't necessary to warm it. Sometimes, if there is space, it is refrigerated overnight and warmed in the oven the next day.

"The guy who gets the last few bites gets crispy critters," Theresa says. Recipe makes 75 small portions.

BOMBE CARTIER

This luscious dessert originated in the *Angel Fire Country Club.*

1 ½ teaspoons gelatin
¼   cup cold water
2   cups milk
1 ½ cups sugar
2   eggs, separated
1   teaspoon vanilla
4   cups whipping cream
18   macaroons
¼   cup Cointreau
1   cup strawberries
     or ½ cup currant jelly

Soak gelatin in cold water. Stir milk and sugar together and bring just to boiling point. Dissolve gelatin in milk mixture. Beat egg yolks and gradually add hot milk. Beat until blended. Stir and cook in a double boiler over — not in — hot water until custard thickens slightly. Cool. Add vanilla. Chill until almost set. Whip the cream until thick but not stiff. In a separate bowl, beat egg whites until stiff but not dry. Fold the cream and the egg whites lightly into the custard. Have ready the macaroons, which have been sprinkled with Cointreau and spread with mashed strawberries or currant jelly. Place alternate layers of macaroons and custard in a large mold. Cover and freeze for 6 hours. Unmold and serve. Serves 15 to 20.

PIES, CAKES
AND COOKIES

NEW MEXICO'S NUTS

In the Portales area, they grow more Valencia peanuts than anywhere in the United States. Around Las Cruces and the Mesilla Valley, the pecan is king — the big, crisp sweet kernels end up in pies, cakes, candies and breads all over the country. And on the dry hillsides throughout the state, people have gathered the wild piñon nuts from the gnarled little pines for thousands of years.

Is it any wonder, then, that New Mexicans love to make desserts using nuts? In this book we've included several favorite recipes using New Mexico's favorite nuts. We hope they'll inspire you to dream up more uses for them yourself.

110

Or perhaps you'll agree with our Pueblo and Spanish recipe consultants who each said, "I don't have time to use them in recipes — we're too busy eating them the way they are."

PEANUT COCONUT PIE

Wilma Skinner's prize-winning pie is made from New Mexico Valencia peanuts from Portales, of course.

4 eggs
1 cup corn syrup
¾ cup sugar
1 teaspoon vanilla
1 cup chopped salted peanuts
1 cup flaked coconut
1 peanut butter pie crust shell

Beat eggs until thick and lemon colored. Gradually add corn syrup, sugar and vanilla, beating after each addition. Stir in peanuts and coconut. Pour into pie shell. Bake at 350 degrees F for 1 hour.

Peanut Butter Pie Crust

2 cups flour
1 teaspoon salt
⅓ cup shortening
½ cup smooth peanut butter
⅓ cup ice water

Sift flour and salt into bowl. Add shortening and peanut butter. Cut into flour until texture of cornmeal. Add water and stir with fork until mixture balls up. Chill. Roll out on floured board. Makes 2 8-inch crusts.

PECAN PIE

¼ cup butter or margarine
½ cup sugar
3 eggs
¼ teaspoon salt
1 cup corn syrup
1 teaspoon vanilla
1 cup New Mexico pecan halves

Cream butter and sugar. Beat in eggs one at a time. Mix in salt, syrup, vanilla and pecans. Pour into deep 8-inch unbaked pie shell. Bake 45 minutes at 325 degrees F. Cool and serve plain or with whipped cream or ice cream. (Don't count your calories today.)

HONEY-NUT PIE

Substitute honey for the corn syrup and add ½ teaspoon almond extract.

PIÑON PIE

Marian Meyer, who is a piñon aficionado, recommends this delectable pie.

1   8-inch baked pie shell
¼ cup real butter
¾ cup brown sugar, firmly packed
4   eggs
1   cup light corn syrup
1   cup piñon nuts
¼ teaspoon salt
1   teaspoon lemon juice

Cream butter and brown sugar. Beat in eggs one at a time until **113** mixture is light and fluffy. Beat in the corn syrup. Stir in nuts, salt and lemon juice. Pour into baked pie shell and bake at 375 degrees F for 30 to 40 minutes. Serve plain or with whipped cream or ice cream.

INDIAN PIES

Sometimes called Spanish pies or flat pies, these are not unlike the currant or raisin squares made in the Highlands of Scotland.

Prepare a double recipe of regular pie crust dough that is not too short. Roll half the dough out into a thin sheet and line a large baking pan or jelly roll pan. Cover the pastry evenly with one of the fillings below or with thinly sliced apples sprinkled with a teaspoon of cinnamon and a cup of sugar, or with any combination that appeals to you. Roll out the remaining pastry and use it for an upper crust. Prick the surface with a fork, brush with evaporated milk or with egg beaten with a little water, and sprinkle with sugar. Bake at 350 degrees F for about 45-55 minutes, or until the pie seems well browned and cooked through the middle. Cool in pan on rack. Cut in squares to serve.

114

Prune Filling

3 pounds pitted prunes
4 cups water
1 cup sugar
1 cup raisins
1 teaspoon lemon juice

Cover the prunes with water, bring to a boil and simmer until tender. Cool slightly and puree. If mixture is too thick, add more hot water. Mix in sugar, raisins and lemon juice.

Apricot Filling

1 pound dried apricots
5 cups water
2 cups sugar
½ cup brandy (optional)

Cover apricots with water and sugar, bring to a boil, cover and simmer until very tender. Cool slightly. Puree the mixture in a blender or food mill. If mixture is too thick to spread easily, add more water. If it's not sweet enough, add more sugar. Mix in the brandy, if desired.

Raisin Filling

2 pounds raisins
4 cups water
2 tablespoons flour
2 tablespoons sugar

Cover the raisins with water, bring to a boil, cover and simmer for 5 minutes. Mix the flour and sugar together in a cup, and blend into the raisins. Bring to a boil again and stir until mixture has thickened. If it seems too thick to spread easily, add a little water.

EMPANADITAS

Rich and delectable, these mincemeat turnovers mean Christmas to many a New Mexico boy and girl. This is Martha Montoya's traditional recipe.

Filling

2 beef tongues
2 cups sugar
1 teaspoon salt
2 teaspoons cinnamon
1 teaspoon allspice
1 tablespoon vanilla
1 cup raisins

1 cup roasted shelled piñon nuts
2 tablespoons blackberry brandy

Cover well-washed tongues with water in a large kettle and simmer until tender — about 1 hour. Cool and peel. Retain 1 cup of the tongue broth. Grind meat in a grinder and place in a large bowl. Add remaining ingredients and mix well with hands, using tongue broth to moisten. Let mixture stand while you prepare pastry.

Pastry

5 cups flour
1 teaspoon salt
3 tablespoons sugar
¾ cup shortening (part lard)
½ cup evaporated milk
½ cup water

Sift flour into a large bowl and add salt and sugar. Cut in shortening. Mix in milk and water to form a soft dough. Knead dough with hands for about 3 minutes. Form dough into balls about 1½ inches in diameter. Roll out on floured board. Place 1 teaspoon filling on half circle of dough, folding over other half circle to enclose. Pinch edges of dough together to prevent filling from leaking. Deep fry empanaditas a few at a time in moderately hot oil (350 degrees F) until golden brown, turning once. Drain on paper towels. Makes about 4½ dozen empanaditas.

Empanaditas taste best when eaten warm. They may be placed on a cookie sheet and reheated in a 300-degree F oven.

BAKED EMPANADAS

New Mexico State University's Cooperative Extension Service is a gold mine of recipes. If you can't eat deep-fried foods, you might want to try their version of baked empanadas.

3 ounces cream cheese
½ cup butter or margarine
1 cup flour
1 cup thick applesauce

Cream butter or margarine with cream cheese until fluffy. Add flour and mix until a smooth ball is formed. Wrap well and refrigerate for at least 4 hours or overnight. Remove from refrigerator ½ hour before using. Roll out dough on a floured board to ⅛- inch thickness. Cut in approximately 3-inch rounds. Place 1 tablespoon of applesauce on each round. Fold over and seal. Flute edges. Bake at 375 degrees F 15 to 20 minutes. Serve warm with a sprinkle of powdered sugar. May be served with ice cream if desired. (This dough is very tricky and hard to handle.)

QUESADILLAS

2 cups cottage cheese
1 egg, beaten
½ cup sugar
1 teaspoon cinnamon
Empanada dough

Sieve cheese and blend with other ingredients. Use as a filling for empanaditas.

LYNE AND MARY'S STRAWBERRY CHEESECAKE

From a popular Truth or Consequences restaurant, we get this easy and tasty recipe.

1 14-ounce can Eagle brand condensed milk
1 8-ounce package Philadelphia cream cheese
⅓ cup lemon juice
1 teaspoon vanilla
1 graham cracker pie crust
2 cups fresh strawberries

Gradually add milk to cream cheese and blend. Then, with a spatula, fold in lemon juice. Add vanilla and turn into pie crust and allow to chill for 30 minutes. Pour strawberries over the top and serve.

PERISCOPE
PUMPKIN CHEESECAKE

A most unusual cheesecake from the noted *Periscope* in Santa Fe.

1 ½ cups zwieback crumbs
3   tablespoons sugar
3   tablespoons melted butter

1   pound cream cheese
1   cup light cream
1   cup cooked pumpkin
¾   cup sugar
4   egg yolks
3   tablespoons flour
1   teaspoon vanilla
1   teaspoon ground cinnamon
½   teaspoon ground ginger
½   teaspoon ground nutmeg
¼   teaspoon salt
4   egg whites, stiffly beaten

1   cup commercial sour cream
2   tablespoons sugar
½   teaspoon vanilla

Combine crumbs, sugar and butter and press in bottom and sides of a 9- or 10-inch springform pan. Bake at 350 degrees F for 5 minutes.

In a large mixing bowl, beat cream cheese until fluffy. Beat in cream, pumpkin, sugar, egg yolks, flour, vanilla, cinnamon, ginger, nutmeg and salt. When mixture is smooth, fold in egg whites. Turn into prepared springform pan and bake at 325 degrees F for 45 minutes.

Combine sour cream, sugar and vanilla and spread over hot cheesecake. Bake 5 minutes longer. Turn off oven and allow cheesecake to cool in oven. Chill and remove from pan to serve.

BAKLAVA

A popular dish at Albuquerque's annual Greek festival.

6   cups walnuts, chopped very fine
1 ⅓ teaspoons cinnamon
½   teaspoon ground cloves
⅓   cup sugar
1   pound sweet butter
1   pound filo*

Mix well: nuts, cinnamon, cloves, sugar. Melt butter. Line 10 x 15 baking pan with filo, brush with butter; repeat this process until 5 or 6 sheets line bottom of pan. Brush sixth layer with butter and sprinkle with nut mixture. Repeat until all ingredients are used. End with 6 or 7 pastry sheets. Trim and cut into diamond shapes. Pour remaining butter over pastry. Bake in 350-degree F oven for one hour. When pastry has browned to a golden color, cover with foil to prevent further browning.

Syrup

2   cups sugar
1   cup water
1   slice lemon
1   stick cinnamon
⅓   cup honey

While pastry is baking, boil mixture to form a thin syrup (20 to 30 minutes). Spoon cool syrup over hot pastry.

*Filo, thin sheets of Greek pastry, may be found in many delicatessen and specialty food shops.

PEANUT BUTTER FUDGE CAKE

Another prize-winning recipe, this from Sondra Hugg.

¼   cup butter
1   cup peanut butter, smooth or crunchy
2 ¼ cups sugar
1 ½ teaspoons vanilla
3   eggs
½   cup cocoa
3   cups sifted flour
1 ⅔ teaspoons baking soda
¾   teaspoon salt
1 ½ cups ice water

Cream butter, peanut butter, sugar and vanilla. Beat in eggs one at a time. Sift together dry ingredients and add alternately with water to mixture. Pour into greased and floured tube pan and bake at 350 degrees F for 1 hour. Cool 20 minutes in pan, then invert on plate. Cool and frost. (Reduce baking soda at higher altitudes and bake in 375-degree F oven.)

Frosting

2   cups sugar
1   cup light cream or evaporated milk
2   tablespoons cocoa
½ cup peanut butter

Mix all ingredients together in a heavy pan. Bring to a boil and cook until it reaches a soft-ball stage. Beat until creamy and spreadable. Add cream if too thick.

PEARL'S SPECIAL CAKE

Pearl Barbour Ditmore of Lovington bakes nearly 300 of these cakes every Christmas and gives them to members of organizations that regularly meet at *Pearl's Dining Room.*

1 cup oil
1 cup fruit juice
  or syrup drained from canned fruit cocktail
2 cups brown sugar
3 eggs
4 cups sifted flour
2 teaspoons baking soda
1 teaspoon salt
2 teaspoons cinnamon
2 teaspoons nutmeg
2 teaspoons allspice
2 teaspoons ground cloves
2 cups broken pecans
2 cups drained fruit cocktail

Grease and flour a tube or Bundt pan. Combine oil and juice. Mix in brown sugar. Beat in eggs one at a time. Sift in dry ingredients and mix well. Last, stir in nuts and fruit. Turn into prepared pan and bake 1½ hours at 325 degrees F.

PAN DE LOS TRES REYES

We had bread for the queen — now we have bread for the Three Kings. Ruth Goodall Fish gave us this recipe many years ago.

1 cup butter or margarine
¾ cup sugar
3 eggs
¼ cup milk
3 cups flour
¾ cup golden raisins
¾ cup currants
4 tablespoons candied orange peel, chopped
4 tablespoons citron, chopped
4 tablespoons chopped almonds
1 teaspoon cinnamon
¼ teaspoon allspice
1 bean

Cream butter and sugar until fluffy. Beat in eggs one at a time. Add milk and beat thoroughly. Coat raisins, currants, citron and orange peel with a little of the flour. Sift rest of flour and spices into batter. Fold in until blended. Add fruits and nuts and mix well. Stir in the bean. Turn into a greased and floured ring mold. Bake in slow oven — 275 degrees F — for about 2 hours.

To serve the cake on El Día de los Tres Reyes Magos — January 6 — place on a serving plate and ring with a wreath of boxwood sprigs, smilax, wandering jew or juniper sprigs. Set a white candle, representing the Christ Child, in the center. Place three candles — one brown, one yellow and one black — in the cake for the three kings. The person who gets the bean in his slice is the king or queen of the festivities and is especially blessed.

PUMPKIN PECAN SPICE CAKE

Pumpkins and pecans make an autumn cake that everyone loves. This is one of Patricia Montoya's specialties.

½ cup shortening
1 ½ cups sugar
3 eggs
1 cup cooked or canned pumpkin
⅔ cup milk
1 ¾ cups flour
½ cup dry powdered milk
2 teaspoons baking powder
1 teaspoon baking soda
1 teaspoon salt
2 teaspoons cinnamon
½ teaspoon nutmeg
¼ teaspoon allspice
¼ teaspoon ginger
1 cup pecans, coarsely chopped

Cream shortening and sugar until fluffy. Beat in eggs one at a time. Combine pumpkin and milk and add to mixture. Sift all dry ingredients together and add to pumpkin mixture. Beat well. Add nuts. Turn into 13x9x2-inch pan that has been lightly greased and floured and bake at 350 degrees F for 40 to 45 minutes. Cool on rack. Frost with lemon or vanilla frosting.

NAVAJO PUBERTY CAKE
(Al Kaad)

Traditionally served during a girl's puberty ceremony, this cake is also made for other special occasions. Larry King brought this recipe to us from his home near Red Rock on the Navajo Reservation.

2   pounds yellow stone-ground cornmeal
1 ½ quarts boiling water
1   cup sprouted wheat flour
1   pound raisins
Cornhusks

Prepare a hole in the ground a little larger than the size of the cake you want and 5 or 6 inches deeper. For the puberty ceremony, a round cake is traditional. Build a fire in the hole and keep it going for several hours. Remove the ashes and embers and brush the cavity clean. Line the cavity with several layers of wet cornhusks. Mix the cornmeal with boiling water, sprouted wheat flour and raisins. Pour the mixture into the lined cavity. Cover with several layers of wet cornhusks, then several layers of newspapers. Put 3 or 4 inches of damp earth above the cornhusks. Build another fire on top of this earth. Don't let the fire go out, but keep feeding it so there are always hot embers. At the end of 8 hours, remove the fire and the earth. Take out the cake, which will be solid. Dust off all earth that clings to the cake. Slice to eat. Remove the cornhusks, which will be like a skin or rind around the cake, before eating.

BISCOCHITOS

This is New Mexico's traditional cookie.

6   cups flour
¼   teaspoon salt
3   teaspoons baking powder
1   pound (2 cups) lard
1 ½ cups sugar
2   teaspoons anise seeds
2   eggs
¼   cup brandy
¼   cup sugar
1   tablespoon cinnamon

Sift flour with baking powder and salt. Cream lard with sugar and anise seeds until fluffy. Beat in eggs one at a time. Mix in flour and brandy until well blended. Turn dough out on floured board and pat or roll to ¼- or ½-inch thickness. Cut into shapes. (The fleur-de-lis is traditional.) Dust with mixture of sugar and cinnamon. Bake 10 minutes at 350 degrees F or until browned.

BISCOCHITOS SANDOVAL

This is the way Teresita Sandoval of Nambe makes her biscochitos.

2 cups lard
   or vegetable shortening
1 cup sugar
2 egg yolks
1 teaspoon baking powder
3 cups flour
¼ teaspoon vanilla
¼ teaspoon liquid anise
½ cup milk

Cream lard and sugar together. Beat in egg yolks one at a time. Mix in flour and baking powder, then flavorings and milk. If mixture is too soft to roll out, add more flour. Roll out on floured board and cut in shapes. (The fleur-de-lis is traditional.) "Bake by smell," Mrs. Sandoval says. Try 375 degrees F for about 10 to 12 minutes, or until they are golden brown.

INDIAN SUGAR COOKIES

Rosella Frederick of Cochiti Pueblo makes these cookies in her outdoor oven. However, they can easily be baked in your kitchen stove oven. They are somewhat similar to biscochitos.

3   cups lard
2   cups sugar
4-5 cups flour
⅓ cup rosé wine
1   egg
Cinnamon
Sugar

Cream the lard and beat in sugar. Beat in egg. Add rosé wine. Mix in 4 cups of flour, adding more until the dough is stiff enough to be rolled out. Cut in circles or shapes. Dip tops in a mixture of cinnamon and sugar. Bake in medium hot oven (375 degrees F) until lightly browned.

SUSPIROS

Here's a delectable way to use the egg whites left over from your flan.

4 egg whites
1 teaspoon vanilla
1 teaspoon vinegar
¼ teaspoon salt
1 cup sugar

Beat egg whites, vanilla, vinegar and salt together until frothy. Add sugar, a teaspoonful at a time, and continue beating until all sugar is used up. Drop by teaspoonfuls on cookie sheet. Bake at 275 degrees F for about 30 minutes — or until lightly golden brown. Leave in oven with door open for 10 minutes before removing. Cool on rack. Dip spatula in hot water to aid in removing cookies from pan. Store in airtight container. Caution: Don't try to make these on a very humid day. Makes about 50 cookies.

CHRISTMAS CIRCLES

1 cup butter or margarine
½ cup brown sugar, packed
2 eggs, separated
2 cups all-purpose flour
¼ teaspoon salt
2 cups pecans, chopped
½ cup raspberry jam

Start heating oven to 375 degrees F. Cream butter or margarine with sugar until light and fluffy. Mix in egg yolks, flour and salt. Form into 1-inch balls. Dip into unbeaten egg whites; remove with fork and dip into nuts. Place 1 inch apart on greased cookie sheet. Make a slight depression in center of each cookie. Bake 5 minutes, press center again; bake 10 minutes longer. Cool slightly. Remove from cookie sheet. Fill centers with jam. Makes about 3 dozen cookies.

DEL CERRO PECAN BROWNIES

The folks at Stahmann Farms, home of the famous Del Cerro pecans, came up with this great brownie recipe.

½ cup sifted flour
½ teaspoon baking powder
¼ teaspoon salt
1 package semisweet chocolate
⅓ cup shortening
2 eggs
½ cup sugar
1 teaspoon vanilla
1 cup chopped Del Cerro pecans

Sift flour, baking powder and salt together. Place chocolate and shortening in top of double boiler and melt over hot water. Mix until smooth and remove from hot water. Place eggs and sugar in a mixing bowl and beat until thick and lemon colored. Stir in sifted dry ingredients. Add chocolate mixture and vanilla and stir until well blended. Pour into 8-inch square pan that has been greased and lined with greased waxed paper. Sprinkle pecans over top and press lightly into batter. Bake at 375 degrees F for 25 minutes. Remove from pan, cool and cut into 2-inch squares. Makes 16 brownies.

FAMOUS ARGYLL SHORTBREAD

The 1800s brought a large influx of British settlers to southern New Mexico — many of them Scots. In their honor we give you this classic recipe for shortbread.

1 pound real butter (2 cups) (no substitutes)
1 cup sugar
3 cups unbleached flour
1 cup rice flour

Cream the butter — and it *must* be butter. This is one place where margarine, lard or Crisco will simply *not* do. The flavor of shortbread depends on butter — preferably unsalted butter. Beat in sugar. Blend in flour and rice flour (available in most health food stores). On a board dusted lightly with flour and confectioners' sugar, pat out the dough to about ½-inch thickness. Cut in 1½-inch rounds and place on baking sheet. Prick each cookie 2 or 3 times with a fork. Chill in freezer or refrigerator for about a half hour. Then pop into a 375-degree F oven. Immediately reduce the oven heat to 300 degrees F and bake for about 20 minutes. The cookies should be golden — but the bottoms should not be browned or burned. Makes about 50-60 cookies. Store in airtight jars or in tightly sealed packages in the freezer.

RICHARD'S GIANT COOKIES

2 ¼ cups flour
1 ' teaspoon baking soda
½ teaspoon salt
1 cup butter
¾ cup sugar
¾ cup brown sugar, firmly packed
1 teaspoon vanilla extract
2 eggs
2 cups semisweet chocolate morsels
1 cup chopped pecans, coarsely chopped

Preheat oven to 375 degrees F. Combine flour, baking soda and salt in bowl and set aside. In another bowl, beat together butter, sugar, brown sugar and vanilla until creamy. Beat in eggs one at at time. Gradually blend in flour mixture. Stir in chocolate morsels and nuts. Measure out ¾ cup of dough and place in center of cookie sheet. Pat out to a 7-inch circle. Bake for about 13 minutes or until light brown. Recipe makes 6 gigantic cookies.

SPRITZGEBAECK

Frieda Reuter is probably the best known cook in Cloudcroft, and little wonder when she turns out such goodies as these.

1 ¼ cups butter
2 ¾ cups sugar
1   large egg, slightly beaten
4 ½ cups flour
1 ½ cups grated hazelnuts
1   teaspoon vanilla extract

Cream butter. Mix in other ingredients. Work into a smooth dough. "Then the dough, you have to let it rest for a couple of hours or overnight, out of the refrigerator. Then you form rings, sticks, circles or question marks (traditional) with it. You have to sprinkle your cookie pan with flour, no grease. Put the cookies on the pan, let them sit for an hour, then bake in the oven about 250 to 300 degrees F till they're light yellow. Then you can sprinkle those little colored things (colored sugar) on top of them."

132

HOLIDAY HONEY COOKIES

Many areas of New Mexico are known for their production of delectable honey. These cookies utilize the honey and New Mexico's tender sweet pecans. You could also use piñon nuts instead of the pecans, if you have them available.

1   cup butter or margarine
1   cup honey
1   cup sugar
1   egg
3   cups flour
2   teaspoons baking powder
2   teaspoons ground ginger
½   teaspoon vanilla
1 ½ cups coarsely chopped pecans

Cream the shortening. Beat in honey and sugar. Beat in egg. Mix in flour, baking powder and ginger. Stir in vanilla. Last, mix in the nuts. Drop by teaspoonfuls on greased baking sheet and bake at 375 degrees F for 12 to 15 minutes.

PIÑON COOKIES

Marian Meyer gave us this marvelous cookie recipe using New Mexico's favorite nuts.

4   eggs
1 ½ cups granulated sugar
½   teaspoon grated lemon rind
2 ½ cups sifted flour
¼   teaspoon salt
¼   cup confectioners' sugar
1   cup piñon nuts

Put eggs and granulated sugar in the top of a double boiler over hot water. Beat with rotary or electric beater until mixture is lukewarm. Remove from water; beat until foaming and cool. Add lemon rind and fold in flour and salt. Drop by teaspoonfuls onto greased and floured cookie sheets. Sprinkle with confectioners' sugar and nuts. Let stand for 10 minutes. Bake in moderately hot oven (375 degrees F) for about 10 minutes. Makes 5 dozen cookies.

SILVER CITY NUGGETS

These crunchy nutty gems are the editor's choice to give any-one the reputation of being an inspired cook. Out of granola? Use more oats instead. Not enough pecans? Use coconut instead. Granola too sweet? Cut down the brown sugar. No brown sugar? Use 1½ cups of white sugar and a spoonful or two of molasses. The recipe is as adaptable as the contents of your pantry.

1   cup butter or margarine (½ pound)
2   cups brown sugar
1   tablespoon vanilla
2   cups granola
3   cups rolled oats
2   cups New Mexico pecans
¼   teaspoon salt

134

Melt the butter and mix in sugar and vanilla. Mix in remaining ingredients. Mixture will be very crumbly. Spoon loosely into muffin tins. DO NOT PACK DOWN! Use 1 to 2 tablespoons in each cup and fill it no more than ⅓ full. Bake at 350 degrees F for 15 to 20 minutes, or until mixture in cups is brown and bubbling. Remove from oven and allow to cool in tins for 15 minutes before popping the cookies out.

CANDIES

MARILYN'S PIÑON BRITTLE

Marilyn Harenberg uses unroasted piñon nuts in her recipe so that the delicate nuts don't crumble.

2 *teaspoons butter*
2 *cups sugar*
1 *cup white corn syrup*
½ *cup water*
2 *tablespoons butter*
2 *cups* unroasted *piñon nuts*
1 *teaspoon vanilla*
2 *teaspoons baking soda*

136

Using 2 teaspoons butter, coat 1 large or 2 small cookie sheets. In large saucepan, combine sugar, syrup and water. Cook, stirring occasionally, until it reaches the soft ball stage or about 234 degrees F. Add butter and nuts and continue cooking, stirring, until it reaches the hard crack stage or 300 degrees F. Syrup will gradually turn a pale caramel color. Quickly remove from heat, add vanilla and soda. Stir rapidly to dissolve and mix well. Immediately pour as thinly as possible onto buttered sheets. Cool slightly and lift up with a knife and pull as thinly as possible.

LAS CRUCES PECAN PRALINES

Use crisp, tender sweet New Mexico pecans for this recipe, of course.

1   *pound light brown sugar*
⅛   *teaspoon salt*
¾   *cup evaporated milk*
1   *tablespoon butter or margarine*
2   *cups pecan halves (½ pound)*

Mix sugar, salt, evaporated milk and butter in a 2-quart saucepan. Cook and stir over low heat until sugar is dissolved. Add pecans and cook over medium heat to soft ball stage (234-240 degrees F), stirring constantly. Remove from heat and let cool 5 minutes. Stir rapidly until mixture begins to thicken and coat pecans lightly. Drop rapidly from a teaspoon onto aluminum foil or lightly buttered baking sheet to form patties. (If the candy becomes too stiff at the last to handle, stir in a few drops of hot water.) Let stand until cool and set. Makes about 44 small pralines.

PIÑON FUDGE

3   *cups sugar*
1   *13-ounce can evaporated milk*
1   *teaspoon vanilla*
½   *cup piñon nuts*

Melt 1 cup of the sugar in heavy pan, stirring with wooden spoon, until dark brown. Add rest of sugar and stir in milk gradually. Cook to hard ball stage (a drop forms a hard ball in cold water). Remove from burner. Add vanilla. Beat until creamy. Fold in nuts. Pour into buttered 8-inch pan. When firm, cut in squares.

PEANUT PATTIES

The Cooperative Extension Service at New Mexico State University uses New Mexico peanuts from Portales for this munchy candy.

2 ½ cups sugar
1   cup milk
⅔   cup white corn syrup
¼   teaspoon salt
1 ½ cups raw peanuts
1   tablespoon butter or margarine
1   teaspoon vanilla

Mix together sugar, milk and corn syrup and bring to a boil over medium heat, stirring constantly until sugar is dissolved. Add salt and raw peanuts and cook, stirring occasionally, until a small amount of the syrup forms a firm ball when dropped into cold water (246 degrees F). Remove from heat, add butter and vanilla. Beat until mixture begins to thicken. Drop rapidly into buttered muffin pans. Let stand until cool and set.

OLD-FASHIONED FUDGE

3 cups sugar
¼ cup corn syrup
3 squares chocolate
¼ teaspoon salt
1 cup evaporated milk (undiluted)
¾ cup Las Cruces pecans

Mix all the ingredients with the exception of the nuts and boil until a soft ball is formed when a little of the syrup is tried in cold water (240 degrees F). Cool until lukewarm and beat until creamy. Add nuts. Spread in a buttered 8 x 8 pan and, when cool, cut in squares.

RUMKUGELN

Cloudcroft's Frieda Reuter suggests making these melt-in-the-mouth morsels at Christmas.

¼ cup butter
2 cups grated semisweet chocolate
2 tablespoons rum
Chocolate sprinkles
2 teaspoons almonds, chopped fine
1 tablespoon raisins

Cream the butter. Blend in the chocolate and rum until mixture is smooth. Divide the dough in half. Make little balls of one half the dough and roll in the almonds. To the other half add the raisins, make into little balls and roll in the chocolate sprinkles. Put the little balls on waxed paper and let them dry. "Very good!"

SCHOKOLADENWURST

German chocolate sausages for Christmas.

3½ cups semisweet chocolate bits
1 tablespoon butter
1 egg, slightly beaten
1 teaspoon vanilla extract
1¾ cups slivered almonds

Melt the chocolate and butter in the top of a double boiler. Mix in egg and vanilla. Then add almonds. Turn out on waxed paper and form into a wurst (sausage shape). Refrigerate for several hours. Cut into little slices.

BUTTER-PECAN FUDGE

5   *tablespoons butter*
1 ¼ cups brown sugar
1 ¼ cups white sugar
1   cup sour cream
1   teaspoon vanilla
1   cup Las Cruces pecans, chopped

Melt butter in heavy pan. Add brown sugar and heat to boiling. Add granulated sugar and sour cream. Cook over low heat, stirring until sugar is dissolved. Cook to soft ball stage (234-240 degrees F). Cool to lukewarm, then beat until stiff. Add vanilla and pecans. Spread in greased 8 x 8 square pan and let cool. Cut into squares.

MISCELLANEOUS

PATE MAISON CARTIER

This family recipe for a country-style paté comes from the chef at the *Angel Fire Country Club.*

1½ cups mashed braunschweiger
1½ cups cream cheese
1   tablespoon gelatin
¾   cup water
1   can condensed consomme
2   teaspoons Worcestershire sauce
¼   cup finely chopped walnuts or pistachios
¼   teaspoon salt
1   pressed clove garlic
1   tablespoon minced parsley
4   dashes Tabasco sauce
3   tablespoons minced pimiento

Blend braunschweiger and cream cheese together with a fork. Dissolve gelatin in water. Bring consomme to a boil and combine with dissolved gelatin. Use 1¼ cups of this mixture to line a 1-quart mold. (Freeze the mold, then dribble in the gelatin mixture, rotating the mold so that all sides get a thin layer of gelatin. Refrigerate until ready to fill.) With a fork, blend the remaining gelatin mixture with all the other ingredients, including the braunschweiger and cream cheese. Work until smooth. Turn the paté into the gelatin-lined mold and refrigerate for 6 hours. To serve, dip mold quickly in hot water and unmold on a cold plate. Cut into ½-inch slices and serve on lettuce with a lemon wedge.

TOSTADOS

Cut fresh or canned corn tortillas into triangles and deep fry in oil at 380 degrees F until they are crisp. Drain on paper towels. Sprinkle with salt. These are the original "corn chips." Use with dips, soups or beverages.

NACHOS

Prepare tortillas as above. While they are still hot, sprinkle with onion or garlic salt and chile powder. Or — sprinkle the chips with grated longhorn cheese, chile powder and garlic salt, then heat in the oven until the cheese melts. Or spread each chip with a bit of mashed beans, season with red chile powder or a bit of fresh chopped green chile, sprinkle liberally with grated longhorn cheese, add a touch of garlic salt and broil until cheese melts.

CHILE CON QUESO

2   tablespoons butter or margarine
1   medium onion, minced
1   clove garlic, minced
1   tablespoon flour
1   13-ounce can evaporated milk
1   pound longhorn cheese, grated
Salt to taste
½-1 cup chopped green chile

Saute minced onion and garlic in butter in large heavy saucepan. Blend in flour with wooden spoon. Add milk and cheese. Stir constantly until cheese is melted and mixture is smooth and thick. If mixture seems too thick to use as a dip, blend in a little water. Mix in the chopped green chile (fresh, frozen or canned) to suit your taste. Serve in a chafing dish with tostados, corn chips or raw vegetable sticks to dip in the mixture.

GAZPACHO NEW MEXICO

A delectable and cooling "liquid salad" from Spain — with a special New Mexico touch.

2 *pounds tomatoes, peeled*
   ***or** 2 14½-ounce cans stewed tomatoes*
1 *cucumber*
½ *green pepper*
1 *large onion*
1 *clove garlic*
¼ *cup olive oil*
1 *tablespoon vinegar*
1 *cup tomato juice*
Salt to taste
1 *4-ounce can diced green chile*
Ice cubes

Dice half the tomatoes, being careful not to lose any of the juice, half the cucumber, half the onion, half the pepper. Set aside in a large bowl or pitcher. Put the remaining tomatoes, cucumber, pepper and onion into a blender, along with the garlic, olive oil, vinegar, tomato juice, salt to taste and green chile. Blend for a few seconds. Pour into container with chopped vegetables. Mix well, cover and chill thoroughly. Serve with 2 or 3 ice cubes in each bowl. Sprinkle with garlic croutons or serve with hot garlic bread. Serves 6 to 8.

HIGH COUNTRY PEA SOUP

2 cups dried green split peas
8 cups water
2 cups diced leftover ham
   or *1 meaty ham bone*
1 clove garlic, minced
1 medium onion, minced
1 clove
1 teaspoon honey
   or *1 teaspoon apricot or peach jam*
1 4-ounce can chopped green chile
Salt to taste

Combine all ingredients except chile and salt in a large heavy pan. Bring to a boil and simmer for 1½ to 2 hours or until the peas are very soft. Add more water while cooking if necessary. Remove the bone, if used. Mix in chile. Add salt if needed (the ham may be salty enough to season the soup). Reheat and serve.

CORNMEAL COFFEE

From the Joseph Lonewolf family of Santa Clara comes this classic recipe for a beverage that can be used as a substitute for coffee.

2 cups blue or white cornmeal
½ cup sugar
½ teaspoon cinnamon
Milk

Brown the cornmeal in a hot (425 degrees F) oven for 8 to 10 minutes by spreading in a thin layer on a cookie sheet and stirring several times to prevent scorching. Mix sugar and cinnamon with the browned cornmeal. Use this mixture like cocoa. Stir into hot milk and simmer for 10 minutes — about 2-3 tablespoons per cup.

FROTHY CHOCOLATE

1 quart milk
2 squares sweet Mexican chocolate *
1 1-inch stick cinnamon
1 teaspoon instant coffee
1 teaspoon vanilla
¼ teaspoon nutmeg

Mix all ingredients into the milk, and heat the milk almost to boiling, stirring constantly. When chocolate has melted, remove from heat. Do not allow mixture to boil. Remove cinnamon. Beat milk with a rotary beater or a *molinillo* until frothy. Serves 4.

*Or use 4 tablespoons cocoa plus 3 tablespoons sugar.

147

SANGRIA

A classic Spanish summer cooler, this wine drink is popular in New Mexico, too. This is just one of several versions.

1 lime
1 lemon
1 orange
½ cup triple sec
½ gallon dry red wine
1 quart club soda **or** grapefruit soda

Slice lemon, lime and orange thinly into large pitchers or a punch bowl. Add the triple sec. Mix in red wine and ice. When ready to serve, mix in the club soda. Serve over ice. Serves 16.

INDEX

WHAT'S THAT WORD?

Tortilla	A thin flat cake made of special blue or yellow cornmeal *(masa harina)* or flour. The tortilla is the basis of many New Mexican recipes.
Taco	A sandwich made of a cornmeal tortilla folded around meat, beans or chese.
Enchilada	A cornmeal tortilla wrapped around or layered with meat, chicken or cheese, and covered with red or green chile sauce.
Burrito	A flour tortilla wrapped around a filling of beans and sauce.
Ristra	A string of chiles tied together to hang up to dry.
Posole	Corn kernels that have been treated with lime; hominy.
Chicos	Dried sweet corn kernels.
Chile pequins	Crushed dried chile seeds.
Masa harina	Specially ground cornmeal for making tortillas and tamales.
Tamál, tamale	Thick *masa harina* wrapped around a spicy meat filling, enclosed in cornhusks and steamed.
Horno	A beehive-shaped outdoor oven of Spanish-Moorish origin, used by Spanish-speaking and Pueblo Indian cooks.
Huevos	Eggs.
Frijoles	Beans (usually pinto beans).
Frijoles refritos	Refried beans.
Piñon nuts	The nuts from the pine cones of the piñon tree.
Tostado	A toasted or fried piece of cornmeal tortilla.
Natillas	Boiled egg custard pudding.
Flan	Baked custard; crème caramel.